SINGING FAMILY *of the Cumberlands*

Jean Ritchie

JEAN RITCHIE

Singing Family

OF THE CUMBERLANDS

THE UNIVERSITY PRESS OF KENTUCKY

Singing Family of the Cumberlands was first published by Oxford University Press in 1955; reprinted in 1963 by Oak Publications and in 1980 by Geordie Music Publishing. Songs are the property of Geordie Music Publishing. Illustrations are by Maurice Sendak.

This edition is published in 1988 by
The University Press of Kentucky

Scholarly publisher for the Commonwealth,
serving Bellarmine College, Berea College, Centre
College of Kentucky, Eastern Kentucky University,
The Filson Club, Georgetown College, Kentucky
Historical Society, Kentucky State University,
Morehead State University, Murray State University,
Northern Kentucky University, Transylvania University,
University of Kentucky, University of Louisville,
and Western Kentucky University.

Editorial and Sales Offices: Lexington, Kentucky 40506-0336

Library of Congress Cataloging-in-Publication Data

Ritchie, Jean.
    Singing family of the Cumberlands / Jean Ritchie.
        p.   cm.
    Originally published: New York: Oxford University Press, 1955.
    Includes index.
    ISBN 0-8131-1679-1 (alk. paper).   ISBN 0-8131-0186-7 (pbk.: alk. paper)
    1. Ritchie, Jean.   2. Folk singers—Appalachian Region—Biography.
3. Ritchie family.   4. Folk music—Appalachian Region.   5. Folk-songs, English—Appalachian Region.   I. Title.
ML420.R6A3 1988
784.4'922—dc19
[B]   88-17337

This book is printed on acid-free paper meeting
the requirements of the American National Standard
for Permanence of Paper for Printed Library Materials. ♾

Contents

TO *the other fifteen:*
Mom
Dad
May
Ollie
Mallie
Una
Raymond
Kitty
Truman
Patty
Edna
Jewel
Opal
Pauline
and Wilmer
This book is humbly and lovingly DEDICATED

Recollections of what folks told me was said and done at my birth, and some early memories of my own, of the family fireside on a winter's night where some true hant tales were told, and ghosty songs sung.

I WAS BORN in Viper, Kentucky, in the Cumberland Mountains, on the eighth day of December 1922. I think I was a little of a surprise to my mother who had thought that if a woman had a baby in her fortieth year it would be her last. Mom had my brother Wilmer when she was forty, and she settled back to raise her thirteen young uns without any more interference. Then when she was forty-four, I came along.

It must have been hardest on Wilmer; he had himself all fixed to be the baby of the family for life. Mom says that the day I was born they found him, in the middle of all the excitement, away out behind the house all alone. He was leaning up against the old June-apple tree just crying his eyes out. He wouldn't tell what was the matter for a long time, but finally he snubbed and said that he never would get to sleep with Mommie no more.

My sisters laughed and made a great joke out of it, and shamed him and said that was a fine way to act when there was a pretty little sister in the house. But Mom told them to hush about it, and she told Wilmer to climb into the bed too. So that first night she slept with her girl babe and her boy babe and my Dad, all three.

Well, that was my introduction to this world, so they tell me, the way families will remember little funny things about a birth or a marrying or even a funeral, and tell about them a thousand times over the years on all those occasions when families start to recall old times. Whenever the Ritchie family falls into one of these sessions of telling tales on one another, it is sure to take up a long evening, because we have so much to remember and so many to remember about.

My very first memory is of our house — filled with crowds and noise and laughing and singing and crying. Beds, chairs, everything full and running over with people. There was never quite enough room even at our long homemade table for all of us to sit and have any elbow room, but we managed to get everybody around it by standing the little ones at the corners. When she saw us all ranged around the table like that, Mom would sometimes say out loud, in a sort of wonder,

'Lordie, it's a mystery to me that the house don't fly all to pieces. I don't rightly know where they all get to of a night.'

Still, our house was thought a big and a fine one in the community, and we were proud of it. My father built it himself with his own hands and the help of the neighbors, and the day he moved his family and his goods and chattels over the ridges with his wagon and team, that was a fine day. Up to this time it seemed he just couldn't find a place he could be satisfied in for long. When they were first married, Mom and Dad went to live in the big old log house with Granny Katty, Dad's mother, on Clear Creek in Knott County, where Dad was born and raised. Two months later Dad finished building their first little house, away up on Clear Creek, and they lived in that until the family got so big that they had to find a place to spread out, farther down the creek. The next move was to the county seat of Hindman, and finally, five or six years before I was born, Dad brought Mom and the big family back to Mom's birthplace, Viper, in Perry County.

Viper is a tiny village whose fifteen or twenty houses string out like a chain around the hillside where it dips inward to follow the curve of the river. There are a few more houses built on the narrow strip of bottom land between the railroad and the river, but not many, for there isn't much bottom land. The mountains are part of the Appalachian chain called the Cumberlands, and in this section they rise in long, gently arching ridges, one following another and one beyond another as far as the eye can see. Because of their shapes they have been given local names like Razorback Ridge, Devil's Backbone, and Longbow Mountain.

To stand in the bottom of any of the valleys is to have the feeling of being down in the center of a great round cup. To stand on top of one of the narrow ridges is like balancing on one of the innermost petals of a gigantic rose, from which you can see all around you the other petals falling away in wide rings to the horizon. Travelers from the level lands, usually the Blue Grass section of Kentucky to the west of us, always complained that they felt hemmed in by our hills, cut off from the wide skies and the rest of the world. For us it was hard to believe there was any 'rest of the world,' and if there should be such a thing, why, we trusted in the mountains to protect us from it.

The place Dad picked out to build our house was the prettiest piece of level land in the community, about three acres stretched out between the hill and the branch. The house when finished was a three-room frame building in the shape of an L, and then they built a separate kitchen in the back yard. In later years this 'old kitchen' was torn down and three small rooms were added onto the long side of the main house, next to the hill, but it was in the first four rooms that the thirteen children were for the most part raised.

We managed it on a sort of dormitory plan. Mom and Dad and the babies slept in the front room that settled back into the hill. The other front room was the girls' room and extended out toward the branch. The boys' beds were in what we called the living room, the third and largest of the three, built onto the back of Mom's room, with a door between. It was here that we received strangers and fine-looking people — peddlers of rugs, herb cures, spices, dulcimers, and tintypes; travelers over the mountains, asking to take the night; and once or twice strange folks from away over the ocean in England, wanting to hear Mom and Dad and the girls sing the old ballads. Then we used the living room. If it was somebody we knew, though, he'd come into Mom's room, first off. That was our real living room.

The very nicest thing about the house to me was the porch that ran all around the house on all sides except the back of the kitchen and the living room where the house settles into the mountain. And my favorite part of the porch was The Corner, where the boys' room met the girls' room and made the ell. The branch, with its water always twinkling and making music, ran parallel to this side of the house, and so did the sledroad up the holler. If you sat in The Corner long, you would most surely see someone go up or down the road, Earl Engle on his mare taking a turn of corn to the mill, or Lee-up-on-the-Branch walking to his house at the head of the holler. He always had a little bagful of something, you never did know what, but it made your mouth water to think what it might be — peppermint or licorice sticks, or hoarhound drops, cinnamon 'belly-burners,' or big round lemon cookies, maybe. Anyway, it was good fun just to watch folks go by, because they always nodded their heads and said 'Howdy-do' to you, same as if you were a grown person.

Mom hated The Corner just about as much as I loved it. It was the handiest place to throw things in passing, and for that reason it was her everlasting despair. She was sure that everybody who passed in the road looked especially into our porch corner and said to himself, 'What messy folks the Ritchies are, plum shiftless, to keep a porch looking like that in plain sight of the road.'

So, about once a week Mom would roll up her sleeves and call around her three or four young uns, and brooms would swish-swash and dust would boil and dogs would yelp and run, and the family would come and admire the clean, empty Corner. Next day Dad would all unthinking throw down a load of wood in The Corner; the little ones would bring their dolls and use the wood to make a playhouse; the boys, Raymond and Truman and Wilmer, would toss their apple and walnut sacks over behind the wood; and the dogs would come in and have pups on the sacks. It was just the most comfortable place in the whole house, and I loved it in the daytime, but Lord pity the poor chap who had to go past it on the way to bed after a long evening spent listening to Granny Katty and Dad and the old people tell stories of ghosts and hants they had seen in their time.

Now, hant tales scared me to death, but I could never keep from listening any more than the ones who had seen the hants could keep from telling them. We would always know when there was going to be hant talk among the old folks. Whenever Granny Katty was staying with us, she'd sit before the fire after supper, and by and by in would come Uncle Philip from down by the river, and after awhile here would be my second sister, Ollie, with her little ones from their house around the hill, and maybe Aunt Maggie would come over, and they all and Mom and Dad would draw up before the fireplace. Then all us young uns would shiver and grin at each other, for we'd know for a fact that the evening couldn't get by without hant tales. Oh, there'd be some weather and crop talk, too, and some singing around, but we waited for that sure quiet minute when someone'd say, 'You hear bout that Wild Thing loose in the woods up behind Grandpa Hall's?' That's when we'd begin scrooching in close to the fire, elbowing silently for good safe places.

Always several of the least ones had to sit on the floor. I

remember I always liked the floor at such times because of the big cracks in the hearth. They were my special secret valleys. While Mom or Dad or one of the visitors was talking, I would act out the tale for myself with things I found by digging with a bent pin into the crack nearest me.

That long rusty needle with a broken eye was a tall bony man, none other than Uncle Shade Ritchie over on Clear Creek. That's where Dad grew up, and where most of the Ritchies still live. If you could judge by the number of tales told to us on those evenings by Granny Katty in her solemn believing voice, more hants have been seen and heard on Clear Creek than in any other territory its size in the world. Whenever Granny told a tale, even the babes listened with their little heads thrown back on their shoulders and their eyes big and round, and their little mouths open just like they understood every word she said.

Then I would forget my needle-man and his oak-splinter horse and would listen to the sound of the thudding hooves of the old roany horse as he and his frighted rider on a wild, dark night got closer and closer to the hanted holler they had to pass to get home. The still, lonesome holler where the THING would hurl itself behind him on his horse and clutch his waist and never make a sound while he lost all power to cry out and his old horse went lightning wild.

And the moment would come in the story when we all stopped breathing, and in that moment it felt to me like I was right there on the horse *with* Uncle Shade, hanging onto the saddle horn. You have never felt such a dread as in that terrible split second when Old Roany was smack in the middle of the hanted holler, *just before the THING leaped on* — then it *did,* the steely hairy arms closed round, and the dreadful race was on. Minutes of silent madness when you shrieked without sound, and the whole world seemed full of guns and cannons that fire and fire with red and blue streaks and smoke but with no breath of noise, only the drumbeats of the wild hooves underneath you somewhere. Until around the roadbend the first cabin light in all these miles shines long and pale across the creek, and the

THING is gone all of a sudden, and you pull on the horse's reins and you find your voice and you give a good long 'Yeeeee-hooooo!' and you feel better. Then you hear Aunt Mol Combs run to her door and say as you fly by, 'Lord, Lord, there goes Shade Ritchie, drunk as a fool again and a-tearing up the Creek.'

Then Granny's matter-of-fact voice saying, 'That tale's so now. Any number people around here'll tell you for a fact that they see It and felt It.' And when I remember how Granny's voice said that, I believe every word of it right now.

The worst thing about hant tales is that they're almost always told in the night, and if you're one of the little ones, you have to leave the circle by the fire and go off to bed about eight o'clock. Just thinking about it, your heart starts to pound out so loud everybody in the house must hear it, and you get cold prickles on top of your head. You know as sure as you're sitting there that just outside that bright circle, in the shadowy back of the room, the hants are waiting to grab hold of you. And if you get by *them,* you still have a long dark way to go to bed. You have to go through the big, damp, cold living room and on out onto the creaky porch with a flickery coal-oil lamp that would just as like as not go out in the gusty night air. Worst of all is passing The Corner, filled with black, fearful movements, any one of which might be the THING ready to pounce on you. Past that, you have to go into the dark bedroom and undress in the cold, crawl in between the icy sheets, and lie there in mortal fear of seeing some awful form pass between you and the window, or of hearing a stealthy turning of the doorknob, and footsteps dragging across the room . . .

No wonder that we kept stiller as it got later, so all the grown people would just keep on talking and forget we were around. We'd grin and punch each other at how well we could fool them, when Mom's voice would crack out like thunder on the Judgment Day, 'Good Land! These young uns ought to've been asleep allus ago. Ollie, look at that poor baby of yourn a-nodding its little head off. Jewel, you and Polly take these two and all of you go off to bed now.'

We'd all holler out at once that we weren't sleepy, and we'd make big eyes to prove it. All the grown people would just laugh, and Dad would say, 'What's the matter, afraid you'll see a sheep's head, like Uncle Joe did the night he foundered on fresh mutton? Lookit them eyes, every one looks like hit's propped open with a matchstick. Begone now and quit sassing.'

Then Ollie would get up and stretch herself and say that she and her crowd had better get home before her man Roy got home from his night job in the L. & N. office at Jeff, two miles down the road.

'Why Ollie, I thought you'd come to take the night.'

'Law no, Mom, I couldn't stay, with all these four little uns —'

'You with no lantern either, and them all scaredy —'

'And you with company. Granny here —'

'We can put beds down like allus. Here, give Jewel that babe, and put that sleepy one on the big bed there, till we get t' others made.'

'Well, I don't know now, Roy —'

'Ah shoot, he'll know where you are. Truman, run out there and tell Roy he's staying all night with us.'

Now let the hants come out of the corners! Ernestine and Helen, Ollie's two oldest, seemed more like sisters than nieces, both of them older than I was. Pauline with the lamp would lead the procession and we'd all jostle and fall over each other getting past The Corner and into the bedroom. But now we'd laugh and jabber and cut up all the way, because there were so many of us the fright was gone. Mom and my sisters Ollie and Mallie would lay out the featherbeds on the floor for us, and we'd lie in the dark and make ghost noises with our mouths, or reach out and tap-tap-tap, soft and low, on the floorboards to make the others think the knocking-spirits were about.

Before long then, one of us would catch everybody quiet and commence singing, down deep in the throat, 'There was an old wooo-oo-man all ski-i-in and bo-oo-ones! OOO-OOO-OOoo!' This was the very scariest song we knew and this was the best kind of a place to sing it, for in the darkness there on the featherbeds there were all manner of ways to put a fright in the others. You could creep your cold hand up and just barely tickle someone's face, or, in a prickly pause in the song, suddenly grab someone by the hair. Or you could creep up from the bed and get over next to the fireplace, slip on a pair of Mallie's shoes and go with dragging footfalls toward the beds, making a dreadful moaning and groaning all the while. Or you could just shudder down into the featherbed, chilling all over with the delicious fright and getting the best scare out of your own singing of it.

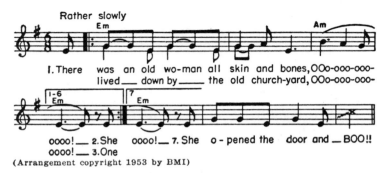

There was an old woman all skin and bones,
   OOO-OOO-OOoo!
She lived down by the old churchyard,
   OOO-OOO-OOoo!
One night she thought she'd take a walk,
   OOO-OOO-OOoo!
She walked down by the old graveyard,
   OOO-OOO-OOoo!
She saw the bones a-laying around,
   OOO-OOO-OOoo!
She thought she'd sweep the old church house,
   OOO-OOO-OOoo!
She went to the closet to get her a broom,

– 11 –

OOO-OOO-OOoo!

She opened the door and

BOO!

At the BOO, we'd all turn wild and scream like panthers in the woods, and raise such a ruckus that Mom would send in to tell us we better settle or Old Rawhead-and-Bloodybones would get us. Now, I never did hear tell of anyone who knew anything about Old Rawhead-and-Bloodybones, who he was, where he came from, or what he would do if he ever did get us, but from the way all the young uns stood around whenever his name was said, I guess he's the granddaddy of the booger-men, and I had my own picture of what he must look like.

Then, out of real respect for Old Rawhead-and-Bloodybones, we'd quiet down and whisper fearfully among ourselves about what we'd do if he caught us. If we got thinking and talking too much about him, Ollie's next-to-the-baby, Kathleen, would begin to cry and we'd have to hush her by singing something not so scary. The best one for that was the song we called 'My Good Old Man' because it was still hanty enough to belong with the good ghosty feeling we all had, and not fearsome enough to make the child cry. We'd let Kathleen say the old man's answers, with someone else's help, because we loved to hear her sweet baby way of saying the words. It made us all laugh and say how smart she was, and it made her happy again.

Where you goin', my good old man, Where you goin' my good old man? My honey, my love, the best old soul in the world.

(Spoken) Goin' to town. What are you goin' to buy there, my good old

Where you goin, my good old man?
Where you goin, my good old man?
      My honey my love
Best old soul in the world?

SPOKEN: GOIN TO TOWN!

What're you goin to buy there, my good old man?
What're you goin to buy there, my good old man?
      My honey my love
Best old soul in the world?

BUY ME A GUN.

What you want a gun for, my good old man?
What you want a gun for, my good old man?
      My honey my love,
Best old soul in the world?

KEEP THE BEARS AWAY FROM YOU.

What d'you want for your supper, my good old man?
What d'you want for your supper, my good old man?
      My honey my love
Best old soul in the world?

BUSHEL EGGS.

Bushel eggs'll kill you, my good old man,
Bushel eggs'll kill you, my good old man,
      My honey my love
Best old soul in the world.

DON'T CARE IF THEY DO.

Where you want to be buried at, my good old man?
Where you want to be buried at, my good old man?

My honey my love
Best old soul in the world?

IN THE CHIMNEY CORNER.

Ashes'll fall on you, my good old man,
Ashes'll fall on you, my good old man,
    My honey my love
Best old soul in the world.

DON'T CARE IF THEY DO.

What you want to be buried there for, my good old man?
What you want to be buried there for, my good old man?
    My honey my love
Best old soul in the world?

SO I CAN SCARE THE DEVIL OUT'N YOUR NEXT OLD MAN!

On the other side of the fireplace wall in Mom's room we could hear the drone of the hant tales being told, with now and again a snatch of song, and after a while we couldn't tell which was the singing and which was the wind making its wintertime sounds around the chimney. We would be fast asleep and dreaming before Ollie and Mallie and Jewel came in and got into the big beds above us. I would rouse enough to hear the laugh in their voices as they talked about the beds.

'Now what would we do if Unie and Kitty and Patty and Edna were home from school tonight?' Ollie would say. And Mallie's answer would run through my half-dream, 'Why, put down a few more featherbeds, I reckon.'

CHAPTER TWO

*Summer twilights on the front porch, where I imagined
myself to be the noble lady of the ballad, followed by
recollections of some very early episodes in my life
which begin to teach me that real life, especially childhood, is a very hard thing.*

I HAVE NEVER been able to decide which times I liked better,
those winter evenings around the fireplace, or the summertime twilights when the song and tale-telling moved out onto
the front porch. Even before I was old enough to take much
part in anything else the grownups did, I was doing my share in
singing the moon up on those soft summer nights.

Dad and the girls and boys would come in hot and dusty from the fields around four o'clock, and we'd all head for the cool willow-hung river that ran around the foot of the mountain down in front of our house. Mom and one or two of the girls would get supper and we'd eat, and then I'd begin work to get everybody out onto the porch. I remember I would always be so afraid that the family would decide *not* to sing tonight, that I would even dry the dishes without being made to. I would keep talking all the while about what a pretty time it was outside, to get them in the notion. But most of the time I need not have worried about it, for by the time the dishes were done, Mom and Dad and the boys would be on the porch, Dad tipped back against the wall in his straight-backed chair, smoking his pipe, Mom swinging and humming gently in the creaky porch swing, and the boys scattered here and there, leaning against the rough bark posts and talking in low tones.

My favorite place on the porch was the swing, in between Mom and whatever sister got there after I did. I loved the lazy motion of the old swing and the way it creaked in time to the music, fast little squawks with the quick tunes, melancholy moans with the slow sad ones. What a safe, warm world it was for me then, leaning sleepily against a soft round arm, watching the darkening air twinkly with lightning bugs.

Mom would say, in between songs, 'Look how big the old Goat-on-the-Hill is tonight! I sure thought I saw him moving along up there.' We all felt friendly with the old goat, Mom and I most of all. The others were apt to laugh at us a little about him. He was made out of a long row of apple trees that stood just on the brow of the hill nearest us. The fore tree being low with a sharp curling branch coming out of the top, it looked like his head, reaching down to crop the tall grasses on the hill. His tail was another small scraggly tree, and this tail switched in a very lifelike manner with every slight breeze. He, too, seemed to keep time, nodding and dancing a little, as our songs drifted up to him from the porch.

And then would come the time when my heavy eyelids

began to droop, and my mind began to wander all around, and the people in the ballads would pass before me out there in the sparkly dusk. The song itself seemed unreal and far, far away, telling dreamily of Fair Ellender and Lord Thomas and courts and processions, love and death, but the people my half-closed eyes saw were alive and beautiful. Fair Ellender rode slowly by on her snow-white horse, her hair like long strands of silver and her face like milk in the moonlight. Then came her waiting maids, dressed all in green and holding their heads high and proud. There was Lord Thomas, tall and brave with his sword shining in his hand, there the wedding folk around the long table. Then, in some easy manner that never had to be explained, *I* became Fair Ellender, and the movement of the swing I sat in became the slow, graceful walking of the white horse. Hundreds of people lined the broad highway as I rode by, thinking I was some queen, as the song wound its way to the tragic ending.

O Mother, O Mother come riddle to me,
Come riddle three hearts as one.
O must I marry Fair Ellender, say,
Or bring the brown girl home?

The brown girl she nas houses and lands,
Fair Ellender she has none.
The best advice I can give you, my son,
Is go bring me the brown girl home.

He dressed himself in scarlet red,
His men he dressed in green,
And every town that he rode through
They took him to be some king.

He rode till he come to Fair Ellender's house
He tingled all on the ring,
No one so ready as Fair Ellender herself

To arise and bid him come in.

O what's the news Lord Thomas, she cried,
What news do you bring to me?
I've come to bid you to my wedding
Now what do you think of me?

O Mother, O Mother, come riddle to me
Come riddle three hearts as one,
O must I go to Lord Thomas's wedding
Or stay at home and mourn?

O moth-er, O moth-er, come rid-dle to me come
rid-dle three hearts as one, O must I mar-ry fair
El-len-der, say, or bring the brown girl home? The
brown girl she has hou-ses and lands, fair ___
El-len-der she ___ has none. The best ad-vice I can
give you, my son, is, go bring me the brown girl home.

There's many a one may be your friend
And many may be your foe;
The best advice I can give you, my daughter,
Is stay at home and mourn.

She dressed herself in a snow-white dress,
Her maids she dressed in green,
And every town that she rode through
They took her to be some queen.

She rode till she came to Lord Thomas's house,
She pulled all in her reins,
No one so ready as Lord Thomas himself
To arise and bid her come in.

He took her by her lily-white hand
He led her through the hall,
He seated her down in the highest place
Amongst the ladies all.

Is this your bride, Lord Thomas, she cried,
She looks so wonderful brown!
You could have married a maiden as fair
As ever the sun shone on.

Dispraise her not, Fair Ellender, he cried,
Dispraise her not to me,
For I think more of your little finger
Than for her whole body.

The brown girl had a little pin knife
It being both keen and sharp,
Betwixt the long ribs and the short
She pierced Fair Ellender's heart.

O what's the matter Fair Ellender, he cried,
You look so pale and wan,

You used to have as rosy a color
As ever the sun shone on.

O are you blind, Lord Thomas, she cried,
Are you blind that you cannot see?
And can't you see my own heart's blood
Come trinkling down to my knee?

Lord Thomas he drew his sword from his side
As he came through the hall,
He cut off the head of his bonny brown bride
And kicked it against the wall.

Then placing the hilt against the wall,
The blade against his heart,
Saying, did you ever see three truelovers meet
That had so soon to part?

O Father, O Father, go dig my grave,
Go dig it both wide and deep,
And bury Fair Ellender in my arms
And the brown girl at my feet.

And so I died, as Fair Ellender, but even death seemed lovely
and romantic in that song; I could imagine how the wedding
guests gathered around as I lay with my pale hair spread about
me on the floor, everybody weeping and saying how beautiful
I was, even in death. I gave myself up completely to wonderful
dreams, forgetting until tomorrow that life was not really like
that. For even though I was only six, I had begun to have my
troubles, and to me they seemed mighty big ones.

The main thing seemed to be that all of a sudden I wasn't
a baby any more. Oh, I got love enough and to spare, but I had
so many grown sisters to mother me and boss me around, that
I was always mixed up about just what I ought to be doing
at any one time. Until I was about five, they had all carried me

on their hips and curled my hair and sung to me, then everybody began accusing everybody else of spoiling me, and from that time on it seemed like they tried to outdo each other picking on me. Any one of them would feel it was all right to give me a slap or a whupping for something, and what would make one of them mad, maybe another would laugh at. All of them teased me, and that made me the maddest of all. I guess that was why they loved to do it so much.

I remember once when I wanted to go into the kitchen house to watch Kitty, Mallie, and Patty get supper, and they took a notion that I'd be in the way. So they locked the screen door and wouldn't let me in. Well, I stood outside of that rusty screen door and looked in. The fire was roaring away in the stove, Mallie was churning by the long table, and the baking bread smelled so good. I begged awhile, then I began to cry and bang my fists on the door. One and another of them kept coming over to the door and laughing at me, pointing their fingers and shaming me. Then finally I heard them make it up among themselves not to let on I was there.

By that time I was so mad I just couldn't stand it, and I determined to get in through that door if it was my last act on earth. I banged and hollered and jumped up and down and kicked the door, and they just sang away and didn't even look. I thought I'd make them look, confound them anyway, so I snatched up an old broom handle lying in the yard and took a runago at the homemade screen door and rammed that stick plum through. It sailed in and rattled around on the floor, and Mallie screamed and nearly turned over the churning of milk. The others stopped singing and came running. I stood, cooled off somewhat but still mad, looking at the hole in the door. I had not really thought to do a trick like that, but when I got started running at the door, I guess nothing on this earth could have stopped me. Lord only knew what would happen to me now. I looked up. They were doubled up laughing and Kitty was holding open the door.

'Come on in. You earned it.'

'What you a-going to do?' — I backed away.

'Just wait till Mommy comes in, that's all. You can set the table. Who'd ever have thought of you a-doing that?'

When Mommy came in from the garden, I hid behind the table. Mom had made that door herself to keep out the flies, and even if it was old and rusty, she wouldn't like to see it finally ruined.

They all told her about it, and for some unknown reason she thought it was funny, too. She said it was time she got after Dad to make a new door, anyway. Then she stopped smiling and said that I had been a very mean girl, and so I would have to finish churning. Mallie got up from the churn and went to frying the meat for supper, and I climbed up on the straight chair by the big white earthen churn and commenced pounding the long wooden dasher up and down. It took both hands it was so heavy, and there was so much milk. My arms got tired out in no time, but Mommy wouldn't let me quit, for she had said I must finish it out, and she couldn't go back on her word. I churned slower and slower. My arms and shoulders ached, and the sorry tears sprang up in my eyes.

'You watch them feet there,' Mom's voice was loud and cross, 'sticking out like that right over the churn. You'll get dirt in my butter. Swear to goodness! Look at them big black feet. If they get much bigger, you going to have to take to wearing your shoes in the summertime, too.'

I hooked my bare feet over the top rung of the chair, for they wouldn't nearly reach the floor, and I bit my tongue to keep from letting on that anyone was making me cry, and I churned harder. Mom hollered out in her calamity voice.

'Look what you a-doing! Swear-r-r-! Sploshing that milk all over the floor. Ruining my clean floor finally and 'fectually and a-wasting all that milk and butter.' Her feet came heavily across the floorboards. I winked my eyes hard trying to see what she was going to do, but my tears were too many. She just looked like a big fat blob. I held fast onto the churn dasher

and waited.

'Listen to her a-snubbin. What you crying about? Being as how you're a-wasting all the milk I'm a-going to have to help you out, but you're going to stay by it until it's done though. Here, you set on my lap and put your hand just above mine, and we'll both churn. Never could stand to hear a young un snub.'

And while she talked a blue streak like that, she wiped my eyes with my dresstail and ran her hands, cool from being outdoors, over my hot, wet, miserable face and settled me in the big crook of her left arm, giving me a secret hug.

We churned. I snubbed once in a while but Mommy kept talking to the time of the churning and my heart began to ease.

'There, now, don't you cry, hush your crying by and by, then we'll make the butter fly, Mommy's baby don't you cry . . .

Churn, churn, make some butter
For my little girlie's supper . . .

    Jean's mad, and I'm glad
    And I know what to please her —
    A bottle of wine to make her shine
    And a pretty little boy to squeeze her!
    A bottle of likker to make her snicker
    And Poppy come home to tease her!
    A bottle of corn just sure as you're born
    And a pretty little boy to squeeze her!
    A bottle of red to suit her head
    And Poppy come home to tease her!

Churn, churn, make some butter
For a little bad girl's supper . . .

    Snake baked a hoecake,
    Set a frog to mind it —

Frog got to nodding and
A lizzard come and stoled it,
   BRING BACK MY HOECAKE YOU LONG-
   TAILED NANNY-O!

Churn, churn, make some butter
For Mommy's baby's supper . . .

     Swing-a-swong, daisy long
     Little blue bird and the sparrow,
     Little doggy burnt his tail
     And has to be hung tomorrow.

    Hush little baby, don't you cry,
    You'll be a big girl by and by.
    Hush little doney-gal, don't you guess,
    Poppy's goin to buy you a brand new dress?
    Hush little baby, don't say a word,
    Poppy's goin to get you a talkin bird.
    If that talkin bird don't sing,
    Poppy's goin to get you a diamond ring.
    If that diamond ring won't shine,
    Poppy's goin to get you a hook and a line.
    If that hook and line gets broke,
    Poppy's goin to get you a nanny-goat.
    If that nanny-goat should go dry,
    Poppy's goin to get you a butterfly,
    If that butterfly fly away,
    Poppy's goin to rock his baby all day.'

CHAPTER   *THREE*

*More childhood troubles. Of my Dad and his hard ways
with us, and of the two outstanding times he took special
notice of me. Punishments and rewards within our
family.*

M Y DAD WAS stern and quiet in his ways, and he hardly
ever laid a hand on us. But we were all dead afraid of
him, for Mom always saved up all our big meannesses to 'tell
Dad, 'never he gets home.' From her fearsome looks whenever
she said this, we knew it would be like the Day of Judgment
if he ever did decide to whup us. Most of the time she did the
whupping herself with the palm of her hand on our behinds
as we ran out of her reach, and so she would generally forget
to tell Dad. But when she did, he would suddenly notice you
across the supper table and it would seem like there was nothing

else in this world but just you and him, with him looking right inside you with those black-brown eyes and with his shaggy eyebrows pulled together. There wouldn't be a blessed sound around the table, and after a while he'd say, dreadfully:

'Now, what'd you do that for? A young un of mine knows better'n that. Now. Dry up. And if I catch you doing a trick like that again and not a-mindin yer Mam, I'll make you wish better, and you'll not forget it in your lifetime.'

That would be all, but I would rather have a hundred of Mom's whuppings and all of her words than these few moments of recognition from Dad. After Dad said a thing like that to one of us, he would look tired all of a sudden, and he'd maybe not speak again through supper. At that time, this was about the only notice he did take of us small children. I can just remember being little enough to be rocked to sleep, and be called the baby still. Then, he'd pet me and trot me on his knee, but when I got big enough to need bringing up, it just seemed like he turned me over to Mom and forgot about me, unless it was to tell me something to go and do, or to quarrel because I didn't mind Mom. Oh, sometimes he'd talk and laugh with us growing ones, or notice us, but that was special. Two of these times stand out in my mind as though they had happened just now. One was when I stumped my toe and he rocked me to sleep, and one was when he wore out seven switches on me.

The late fall day when I stumped my toe was one I won't ever forget, because about the whole end of my left big toe got knocked clean off when I hit it against a sharp rock in the yard. I hollered out like I was dying, and Mom ran out of the kitchen door, scared to death. She thought I was sure killed when she saw all that blood flying, and she clapped her dishrag over my foot. The fresh pain from the soapy rag nearly did kill me, and I was crying so earnestly that I would lose my breath at the end of every bawl I let out. I was kicking and clawing every which way, and Mom was trying her best to hold me to see what on earth had happened. Finally, the first pain settled enough so that I could sit still, and Mom took me into the kitchen and washed my foot and worked on it until she got it to stop bleeding. We had another battle while she poured iodine into it, then she wrapped the toe up in so many white rags that it looked like I had three or four big toes in the one place. I was a good-sized girl then, seven or so, old enough to go to school, and she said I wouldn't have to go back to the schoolhouse after dinner that day.

Pretty soon Dad came home for dinner from Bowman-Watts' Store up at Viper, where he had a job then as a store clerk. Mom told him about my hurt, saying that it was a shame for a young un to have to go barefooted so late in the year, anyway.

Dad made her unwrap the rags, and he looked at my toe. He asked me if it hurt bad. Then he said to Mom, smiling like he wanted to tease her, 'Well, 'pears like the damage is done, now, and she couldn't wear a shoe on that there foot for a few days even if she — wanted to. Maybe by the end of the week . . . Well, I've got to hurry back to work and let Sam go get his dinner.'

That evening when he came back home, he walked straight over to where I was sitting on the edge of the bench by the table and swooped me up and held me high until my head grazed the loft boards. He didn't usually play like that with me, and I was so scared I started to cry. I thought he must be out of his mind. Then he said, still holding me high, 'Want me to beard you?'

I screamed, laughing, 'No! No! Mommy, make Poppy stop. He's a-going to beard me!' But I knew it was no use. I hid my face and fought with him, though, because it was fun. This was our favorite game we had played when I was little enough to be petted. He hugged me so tight that I couldn't move a muscle, and he put my head back and rubbed his stubbly jaw all over my face and neck, while I just screamed and laughed. Then he set me back on the bench.

Mom and Mallie were setting supper on the table, smiling the both of them. Wilmer sat in the corner on the bench, looking ashamed and mad.

'Huh,' said Mallie. 'Never saw a young un get so much spoiling in my life.'

'Won't be able to stand her for a week. Big-headed, he's a-making her,' said Mom.

'Baby!' Wilmer whispered.

After supper I dried the dishes, favoring my sore toe as I walked from the big dishpan to the cupboard. Then everybody settled down at one thing or another in the front room, except for me, and I went and sat down on the high porch steps, aiming to watch the half-moon rise in the early dark. I leaned my back against the rough bark of the porch post and looked up at the bright place behind the ridge across the river, and I had a lonesome feeling. I wished for the girls all to be home from school so we could sing the moon up. It was just such a night, but it was hard to sing with just Mom and Dad and Mallie and Wilmer and me. My toe had stopped hurting bad. It throbbed pleasantly. I watched the brightening sky and was proud that I could feel the frail beauty of it. I felt proud of my sore foot and of my lonesome feelings. I felt proud that I was who I was. I wondered if anyone would ever understand how much was in my mind and heart. I wondered if ever there'd come somebody who would know. You couldn't talk about such things. You had to talk about corn and dishes and brooms and meetings and lengths of cloth and lettuce beds. If you should start to talk about the other things — the things inside you — folks might think you were getting above your raising. Highfallutin. Maybe I was the only one. Maybe nobody else in this world felt the things I felt and thought the things I thought in my mind.

'This is the middle of the world,' I said it out loud, low. 'Right here where I'm sitting on this second step is the very middle. And when I get up and go into the kitchen the middle goes too. If I was to sail across the waters, it would be just the same. Nobody else can be in the middle with me, not in the *very* middle. I'm by myself. Alone, alone!'

The screen door shut behind me and I came to myself and hushed quick. Dad walked back and forth, searching the heavens with knowing eyes.

'She won't rain tomorrow, I guess. Be a good day for the field.' He kept walking to and fro behind me. He took out his red handkerchief and blew his nose, making a fuss about it. He kept walking. He whistled a catch of something or other.

'Yep. Be a cler night. A little dew. No frogs a-hollering,' he said.

I spoke up, bold as I could, 'The moon yonder's a-coming up.'

He stopped walking behind me. Finally, he said, 'Your foot feel bad now?'

'It thobs some.' He stood still and hummed a small tune.

'Do you know now what Poppy has brought his babe?' The words were strange to my ears and I could not answer. He pulled out of his britches pocket a piece of brown paper and unwrapped it in the light of the new-risen moon. It was a round piece of chocolate candy and I knew there would be a white or pink creamy inside. It was about the size of my big toe. He thrust the paper at me.

'Here, take it. Poppy has brought his babe a new toe!'

Then he got me on his lap in a straight-back chair and asked me if I was sleepy.

'He's a-ruining her finally and 'fectually,' I heard Mallie say.

We rocked thumpity-whack in the straight chair, there on the porch in the moonlight, and by and by Dad commenced to sing 'Twilight A-Stealing,' an old hymn he had learned in singing school years ago, and one with which we always began our singings on the porch. He hadn't more than got started on the second line in his lonesome shouty voice, before out came Mom and Mallie. Then, finally, Wilmer slipped out, too, and he put in a low part. It was almost like the girls were there!

Twilight a-stealing over the sea,
Shadows are falling, dark on the lea.
Borne on the night wind, voices of yore
Come from the far-off shore.
Far away, beyond the starry sky,
Where the love-light never, never dies,
Gleameth a mansion filled with delight,
Sweet happy home so bright.

Voices of loved ones, songs of the past
Still linger round me while life shall last,
Cheering my pathway while here I roam
Seeking my far-off home.
Far away, beyond the starry sky,
Where the love-light never, never dies,
Gleameth a mansion filled with delight,
Sweet happy home so bright.

Twi-light a-steal-ing ov-er the sea, shad-ows are fall-ing

dark on the lea, Borne on the night wind, voic-es of yore,

Come from the far - off shore. Far a - way be -

yond the star-ry sky, where the love - light nev-er nev-er dies,

gleameth a mans-ion filled with de-light, sweet happy home so bright.

Come in the twilight, come, come to me,
Bringing sweet message over the sea.
Lonely I wander, sadly I roam,
Seeking my far-off home.
  Far away, beyond the starry sky,
  Where the love-light never, never dies,
  Gleameth a mansion filled with delight,
  Sweet happy home so bright.

The other time I remember when Dad noticed me especially
was about a year later, and it was the time he wore out the
seven switches on me. Dad was like all the rest in this way,
that sometimes we could tear down the house and put it
in the loft, as the saying goes, and he would not even let on
that he saw us. Other times just the least little thing would set
him to bellowing. Like the time I wouldn't say 'please' at the
table.

The girls were home from Pine Mountain, Edna and Jewel
and Pauline, and there was Raymond, Kitty, and Patty from
Berea College. Truman was home then, too, working in a
store two miles away, and still single at the time. And of course
Mom and Dad, and Mallie, Wilmer, and me.

It was dinnertime on a rainy day. We children were all laughing and cutting up because in secret we were glad it was raining, and we didn't have to work in the fields. All except Dad,
and he acted mad about it, not saying much through dinner.
He was hard of hearing, anyway, so he always kept quiet when
we were together and hollering all at once, because he couldn't
make head or tail out of what was said. 'If you want me to
understand and answer,' he used to say, 'speak one at a time, and
plain, like decent folks ought. You don't have to yell either.'

I wanted a piece of corn bread. There was one round pone
of bread on the table, and it was away at the upper end by Dad. I
tried several times but I couldn't make a soul hear me. The noise
was making me feel good anyway, and so finally I sang out,

'Gimme the bread, I said!'

Jewel, sitting next to me, turned around quick. 'Don't you know how to ask for anything? If you were to ask for the bread that way at Pine Mountain you'd get sent right home from school.'

'Berea, too,' Patty had overheard. She had her hand on the bread plate. 'Say it nice and I'll pass it.'

I began to get mad. 'How can I ask nice when you're all making so much noise? And this ain't Pine Mountain, and you-all ain't my bosses.'

'She knows how to act,' Mom soothed. 'Say please for your sisters, honey.'

'She don't have any manners at all. She wouldn't know how to be polite if she wanted to,' Wilmer threw in his bit.

I began to blubber and cry to myself. Just because they'd all come fresh from fancy schools was no reason for them to pick on me like that.

'It's time you learnt to be a lady,' Kitty entered in. She spoke as though she knew how to settle all this foolishness. 'We been away too long, that's what, and Mam and Mallie's let her do what she wants. Time she started to grow up in her head to catch up with that big clumsy overgrown frame of hers. Now, sit up like a lady and say, "Please, Patty, will you kindly pass the pone of bread?" '

'No clumsier'n you are!' I wailed. 'I just — wa-want some b-br-EAD!'

Everybody at the table was looking at me and admonishing me but Dad, and he was placidly chewing away, hearing nothing amiss, staring out at the rain falling gray and steady in the back yard. When I started to cry out loud, though, he looked around and saw we were all quarreling.

'Settle, settle here! Mam, what on this earth are you all fussing so for? And what's that one bawling her eyes out about?'

'We were just trying to teach her some manners. How to act at the table,' Kitty said to him.

'What is it you want her to do?' he said.

'To say please. Just one simple little thing. Just to say please,' said Patty.

It was pretty hopeless for me now. Dad had not heard what had gone on before; he couldn't know I was partly in the right. *I* thought so, anyway. And he surely wouldn't listen to me if I tried to make him understand the whole thing. I waited, snubbing.

'Dry up!' Dad commanded. 'Now you say please. The girls are a-trying to teach you something for you own good, and you for one time and season better not be stubborn about it. What makes you so stiff-necked? I told you to dry up. Now, say please!'

If I said it, I'd never hear the last of it from all the others. On the other hand I knew Dad would never listen to me, and I couldn't explain, choked up as I was. But I decided to take a long chance and try. I said some things, not making much sense even to myself. I mumbled and snuffed, looking down at my plate. Dad suddenly rose up from his chair and it seemed to me he leaned all the way down that long board and hung over me.

'Are you a-talking back to me? What did she say? Did she say please? Listen, you little sasser, the only word I want to hear out of you is please. Are you a-going to say it?'

I shook my head, dumb and blind. I had gone too far anyway. They could do anything they wanted to but I wouldn't give in.

I heard Dad push his chair back with a mighty scrape. I heard him muttering, 'Bet you five dollars I will make you say it. Always said I wouldn't raise a young un that wouldn't mind me when I talked to it, and I don't aim to.' I heard him stomp out of the house.

Edna put her arm around me. 'It'd be better if you'd say it and get it over with now,' she begged. She looked scared.

Mom cleared her throat, and when she spoke her voice was trembly. 'Why, I never saw Balis so mad, I don't believe. Lordie mercy, why it's untelling what he'll do and him so franzy like that.'

'Such a fuss about nothing! I won't stay around here while you-all act so foolish,' Raymond said. He got up and left the house.

'Now we'll see who's the boss around here, little girl!' Wilmer was gleeful. He rocked himself back and forth on the bench. I made a vow to myself that if I lived through this, the very next time I caught him out I'd hit him with the biggest rock I could throw.

Dad stayed out in the yard the longest time, while they all reasoned with me to give in. Some said they didn't care a bit if I didn't say it, that I had been spoiling for a good whupping for a long time anyway. Mallie always foresaw the worst, and she said, in a voice of doom, that Dad would half-kill me. She could tell.

Dad came in. He made straight for me. He had a big bundle of apple-tree switches under his arm. Mom jumped up in front of him.

'Balis, Balis, them switches not keen enough. Get willer limbs if you going to whup her. Better to cut than to club and bruise.'

'Stand back now. You raised her so well, whyn't you make her mind? When I do a thing I don't want nobody telling me how.' I was yanked out of my chair onto my feet. Dad shook me until I couldn't hold up my head.

'I give you one more chance. Are you a-going to say it? Are you?'

I swear that I couldn't have said it then if it was the last thing I was given to do on earth. For now a funny feeling had come over me. I was as white shaking mad as he was, and I didn't care if he did beat me. I didn't care a snap of my fingers if he knocked me down and whipped me until the sense left me; I think I even hoped he would. I wanted savagely to feel all the pain he could give me, I wanted once and for all to know the end of his power. I didn't know why I felt this way, but I can remember that I did and that I took time in my mind to be surprised at myself for it. And then I felt like laughing. He took me out on the front porch and started in, and all the time my body felt the blows falling, my mind was feeling freer and freer. And all the time I was yelling bloody murder, screaming and kicking and biting him to make him madder so he would beat me more.

We had it round and round for about half an hour, seemed like. He'd use one switch until he had worn it down to a stump, and then he'd catch up another and begin again with hardly a break in the timing of it. The other children were huddled in the front room watching through the window. I don't know where Mom had got to. Along about the middle of everything, our neighbor Luther Brashear passed by in the road with his mule and sled.

Luther looked up and saw what was going on, and he pulled on the lines and stopped the mule and wrapped the end of the lines around the corner post of the sled. His Dad had given him what everybody thought was the whupping to end all whuppings a week or so before this, and I guess he got fun out of seeing someone else get it too.

Dad ran out of switches. Sweat was pouring down his face and from all over him. His clothes were wet. Mine were too. I fancied they were wet with my own heart's blood. I lay on the floor, still kicking and yelling, still mad. Dad leaned against the house wall and wiped his face. He looked down at me, and he was still mad too.

'Had enough for a while? Did you say it? Are you a-going to?' He was so out of breath he could hardly talk. I was glad of it. I shook my head and cried louder.

'What in the devil is this young un made of?' he thundered. 'I never had a mule brute that could out-stiff-neck you! But I'll outdo you yet, you heifer you. And don't start thinking that I've done all I can do to you neither. I'll get you over your stubborn meanness if it's my last act.'

He grabbed me up and his arms when they touched my sore skin felt like hot searing irons. My whole backsides, from my neck down to my feet, were swelling up and throbbing. Dad got me to the end of the porch where the house was backed against the mountain, and he stepped off this low place and went to where Mom had a little bed of white tearoses planted. The bushes were full of tender buds, and some had just begun to open. I remember it well. Since then the smell of roses has made me think of pain and smart, along with all the sweet things they remind me of. Dad held onto me so I wouldn't run away and he bent over and plucked one of the rose briers up by the roots. Then he carried me back to the porch. I was heavy and he was puffing with the load of me, and every step he took he made the little white roses dance up and down in front of my face. Some of their thorns were new green and tender, but some were brown and hard and very sharp. When he began to beat me with this switch they cut like knives into my skin and laid my back open under the thin dress I wore.

All of a sudden Mom was there and she was crying about as loud as I was. 'Balis, I can't stand it longer, I can't stand to see my baby all tore up like that. She's so little and she's just eight year old. Stop it! Stop it now!'

'I'm not a-stopping till she says what I told her to say.' Dad gritted his teeth together and kept on coming down with the rosebush. By this time I couldn't feel the lashes at all, and could only tell from hearing the swishes and whacks that I was still being whupped. I just yelled from habit, and I was beginning to get awful hoarse. Mom tried to grab the switch.

'Dad, for the Lord God, do you want to kill the young un? Ever bit and grain of her? How can you expect her to say anything when you making her holler like that ever breath?' Dad stopped a minute. Mom leaned over me. I moaned because I couldn't scream any more. Mom straightened herself up.

'There, she said it now and I hope you're all satisfied.' She didn't look any more at Dad, and she picked up what was left of her poor little rose brier and broke it in two and threw it into the yard, saying it was a pity how some people didn't have the sense they were born with. She hollered at Luther to get along home and stop gawking where he had no business, and didn't he know enough to get in out of the rain?

The anger was all gone out of me and I couldn't seem to want to do a thing but lie there on the porch with the rain blowing in cool on my boiling body. I couldn't stand to be touched on the mass of red welts, and I tried in a feeble way to fight Mom off, but I was too tired. The others came out then, and they all seemed sorry that I had got such a whupping. Mom sent them after soap and warm water, and that old iodine for the cut places, and lard to rub on the welts. But then she thought about our lard being salty and that it would make my back worse, and she was casting about in her mind as to what she could find in the house. Then here came Wilmer holding out a box of Sayman's Salve from his case of products he had been peddling among the folks around. The salve was sweet and smooth, and after a while I began to feel better.

But I had a secret I couldn't tell. Only Mom and I knew, and we didn't call each other's mind to it. *I hadn't said please!* Some days later I did tell it to the others, but we kept it from Dad until we knew good and well he was over his mad spell.

I guess that's about the sorest I've ever been. I moped around the house two or three days and it felt good to have everybody sorry for me for a change. That first day and night I had to lie on my stomach in a bed to myself, and I was so feverish hot that I couldn't sleep at all. Mom would come to me in the night and fan me and blow breath on me to try to cool me off. I wanted her to rock me and sing, but she couldn't rock me because of my tender skin, so she sat awhile in the moonlighted window by my bed and made the mattress go up and down with her hand, and she asked me what it was I would like most to hear. I said the one about the Darby Ram, because I was hurt. It was the song she always seemed to pick to sing when any of us got hurt and ran to her. Sometimes she would sing the song and then drift into telling about her own mother and how she had sung the same song to *her* children.

'The Darby Ram' was Grandmother Hall's lullaby song,

my Mom would tell me, and that she could hear Grandmother singing it more than any other. Her given name was Patty, and she was gentle-natured and laughing, and had a beautiful face and a lot of wavy dark-brown hair. That's about all Mom could remember of her, for she died early, in childbirth, when my Mom was still 'little Abbie,' child enough to be rocked on her mother's lap, and smiled down at, and sung to when she was sleepy or hurt. Abbie sang this song then with its bright memory to all her many babies, and the love and the remembering in her voice made it a very special song for all of us. I was never able to frown or cry very long, no matter how angry or hurt, when Mommy put her comforting arms around me and sang with reverent humor about Darby's funny old ram, the wool on whose belly dragged nine miles on the ground, and on his back reached up to the sky for the eagles to nest in, and 'every foot he had covered a half an acre of ground!'

> I went down to Darby's house
> On a market day,
> There I spied the finest ram
> That ever was fed on hay.
>   Fol lol day,
> Fol lol diddle lolly day.
>
> The first tooth he had
> Held a hundred of a horn,
> The next tooth he had
> Held sixty barrel o'corn.
>
>   Fol lol day,
> Fol lol diddle lolly day.
>
> Four feet he had,
> Four feet stood on the ground,
> And every foot he had
> Covered a half an acre of ground.

1. I went down to Dar-by's house on a mar-ket day,
There I spied the fin-est ram that ev-er 'as fed on hay. Fol lol day,
fol lol did-dle lol-ly day. 2. The first tooth he had held a
hun-dred of a horn, the next tooth he had held
six-ty barrel o' corn. Fol lol day_____ fol lol diddle lol-ly day.

Fol lol day,
Fol lol diddle lolly day.

The wool on the ram's belly
Drug nine miles on the ground,
I went down to Darby's house
And stole a thousand pound.
Fol lol day,
Fol lol diddle lolly day.

The wool on the ram's back
It reached up to the sky,
The eagles built their nests there,
You could hear the young uns cry.
Fol lol day,
Fol lol diddle lolly day.

The one that cut his throat
Got drowned in the blood,

The one that held his head
Got washed away in the flood.
Fol lol day,
Fol lol diddle lolly day.

CHAPTER FOUR

*I begin to get to know my Father, and learn what a re-
markable man he is. One of the many tales he told me
about his boyhood, this one being about how he heard
the fiddle played for the first time, and how he himself
learned to play.*

SOMETHING HAPPENED with that whupping that I'm just
beginning to realize. As I think about it now, having put
it out of my mind for so many years, I see that my real com-
panionship with my Dad, my real love for him, got started soon
after that. The big fear was over and gone — I guess I knew
that Dad had done as much hurt as he could ever do to me,
and I knew, too, that he would never do it again. I got so I
wasn't afraid to talk to him, ask him things about my school
lessons, and even tease him a little. It seems now that with

that one big battle we discovered our close-kin personalities, and we began, all unconsciously, to seek each other's company.

My first discovery about Dad was that he was a fine singer. Somehow people had always got the idea that Mom was the big singer of the two, but I soon found out that Dad had hundreds of songs from his growing days, old story ballads, love songs, fun songs, dancy songs, that he never used to sing for any of us children because we didn't know he knew them. The way I began to find out about his songs, I'd ask him to sing 'Darby Ram,' or one or another of Mom's songs, and he'd study awhile and say, 'Well, now, I don't think I rightly know the words straight to that'n. But do you know the one about Old King Cole, him that eat corn bread till his head turned red?' And then he'd light out on one of his play songs that I had never heard before, and he'd remember just how the game was played, too, and describe it to me.

' "Old King Cole," now, we called that one a gettin-up tune. You see, when the chaps and girls used to meet up on a Saturday night for the plays, sometimes it'd be ever so long before we'd get the party started, everybody was so bashful. Maybe one feller'd be braver than the others, and he'd want to hurry things up, so he'd get his girl and they'd cross hands and go marching up and down the floor singing "Old King Cole," and by the time they come to the part about "we'll open up the ring and choose a couple in," why another couple'd be ready to join in, and they'd keep on like that until they had five or six couples up, enough for a set or a regular play-game.'

> Old King Cole was a jolly old soul
> And this you may know by his larnin,
> He eat corn bread 'til his head turn red
> And his old yaller cap needs darnin.
>
> My pretty little pink, I once did think
> That I and you would marry,
> But now I've lost all hopes of you
> And I ain't got long to tarry.

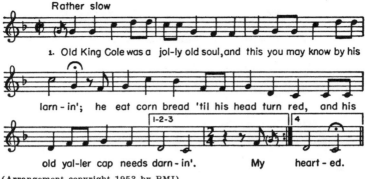

Rather slow

1. Old King Cole was a jol-ly old soul, and this you may know by his larn - in'; he eat corn bread 'til his head turn red, and his old yal-ler cap needs darn - in'. My heart - ed.

I'll take my knapsack on my back,
My musket on my shoulder,
I'll march away to Mexico,
Enlist and be a soldier.

Where coffee grows on the whiteoak trees
And the rivers they run brandy,
Where the boys are pure as a lump of gold
And the girls are sweet as candy.

You may go on and I'll turn back
To the place where we first parted,
We'll open up the ring and choose a couple in
And we hope they'll come freehearted.

And then I found out how wonderful it was to get him started talking about the old days when he was a little boy, and about his mother and dad and their mothers and dads. Since that time I have learned much about our family story and singing from him and have treasured it up. What a lot of things he knew! Not just about the family but about a multitude of outside doings in the world. He had his main education in a one-room log schoolhouse from the old Blueback Speller, and when I would bring my schoolbooks home, along about when I was in the fourth or fifth grade, he would thumb through them and make light of them.

'Why, I learnt all that's in here in the primer class!' he'd scoff. 'That old speller was the only book we had but it had pretty nigh everything there is to know in it.'

Then we'd beg him to spell out a word for us by syllables, the way he'd learned in school. He'd take a long word like incomprehensible and rattle it off, calling out each syllable and linking it to the ones that had gone before, all the way to the end of the word. We'd all fall over laughing and try to do it ourselves, but we'd not manage it nearly as well as Mom and Dad.

'Incomprehensible. I - n - in - c - o - m - com - incom - p - r - e - pre - incompre - h - e - n - hen - incomprehen - s - i - si - incomprehensi - b - l - e - bul - incomprehensible.'

When some of us tried to make everybody be quiet so we could get our lessons at night, Dad and Mom would say to one another:

'What about how they a-doing things now! Used to be in the schoolhouse the teacher wouldn't think we were doing a thing unless we all studied our lessons out loud all at once. He'd walk up and down twixt the seats with his stick and be sure that every chap had his book open and was reading it out loud. Sounded for all the world like a hive of bees. Ever-who read out the loudest was the best scholar.' Dad would chuckle. 'When I was sure he couldn't hear what I was reading I would say all manner of foolishment instead of reading what the speller said. I knew that thing by heart, anyhow. I'd say over little foolish jingles and dancing songs, and pat my feet, but not too loud. It was a good way to study.'

Once, when we got to talking about those days like that, Dad remembered for us the first day he ever heard the fiddle played. He was a little slip of a boy, he said, about nine years old, and he was going to school to old man Nick Gerhart. They got through reciting their lessons and they were all humming through their study, when Maggard Ritchie came in.

'He'd been off somewheres, courting in Virginny, and he

had brought a feller home with him, and they had come down to the schoolhouse to visit with Nick. Nick told the scholars to study away while he talked with the men, and for us not to look up. But you know that stranger had a fiddle in his hand, first one any of us had ever seen, and pretty soon he propped it in the cradle of his arm here and begun to play that thing. Lordie! I thought that was the prettiest sweepingest music. I hadn't heard a sound like that in my life before me, and it seemed like the only thing I'd been a-waiting for all this time. I wanted to holler and jump up and down. I just couldn't mortally stand to sit still on that log bench and that tune snakin around so. No sir, that was one tune that didn't stay in one place no time atall. I was hot and itching all over myself, and I thought to my soul I was going plum crazy. You could hear feet a-stomping all over the house, benches a-screaking, young uns a-giggling, and nobody a-studying fit for a dog.

'Finally I let out a yell and lept off'n that bench and commenced to dance and clog around. Everybody hollered out a-laughing, and some of the other boys jumped up, too. Teacher didn't even try to hold us, he was grinning and patting, too, and having the hardest kind of a time standing anyways still. That man played that tune over and over, and then he played some others and every time he'd touch that bow to them strings, hell would tear loose in that schoolhouse. Us young uns turned summersets, and stood on our heads, and whacked each other over the head and ran about over the log benches, and danced and hollered and cut up — it was a sight to see.

'After a while Maggard and that feller left, and the teacher tried to settle us, put us back to our books, but I couldn't even see the print in that speller. I kept seeing that old fiddle bow race around on "Shady Grove." We around there had always sung that tune middling fast, hopped around to it a little bit, but that fiddle had tuck out with that'n like the Devil was atter her. I was so tickled about that I kept laughing and wiggling round in my seat, and saying the words to "Shady Grove" out loud instead of my lesson.

Cheeks as red as a bloomin rose,
Eyes of the deepest brown,
You are the darlin of my heart,
Stay till the sun goes down.

Shady Grove, my little love,
Shady Grove I know,
Shady Grove, my little love,
Bound for the Shady Grove.

Shady Grove, my little love,
Shady Grove, my dear,
Shady Grove, my little love,
I'm goin to leave you here.

Shady Grove, my little love,
Standin in the door,
Shoes and stockins in her hand

And her little bare feet on the floor.

Wisht I had a big fine horse,
Corn to feed him on,
Pretty little girl stay at home,
Feed him when I'm gone.

Shady Grove, my little love,
Shady Grove I say,
Shady Grove, my little love,
Don't wait till the Judgment Day!

'Well, sir, that day I vowed and declared that I would learn to play that fiddle. I didn't know how a little shaver like me could ever get to one, but some day and some way I would, and I'd play just like that stranger from Virginny. And I did, too. I don't guess I ever played as well as he did, but I played when I was growing, enough to play for sets around on Saturday nights at a party. And I didn't learn until I was seventeen or around there, kept it in my mind all that time though, and got around one whenever I could. It was right funny how I finally did learn to do it.

'I had two pretty white geese that kept running off up to Elic's, farther up the creek, and I got afraid they'd take up there and lay eggs and never come home. So I struck up the creek one day to catch them. The sun was hot and I was lazy, so on the way I run across our little young filly mare that was standing in the road, and I just jumped on her back to save walking, and we moseyed along up to Elic's house. We had been working on that filly, breaking her in to ride, and I thought, says I, this would be good practice for her anyways.

'Well, I put her in the yard, and I run my geese down, got back on my mare, and Elic, he came out and stuck my geese under my arms for me, one under my right and one under my left, so I didn't have a hand to hold onto the mare with. But she was feeling the heat, too, and we got along fine and slow.

Road went right through the creek bed for most of the way, and the water was low with the dry spell. Come to a place where the waters were holed up and the horse's feet hit that pool with a splash. Threw up spray and my geese got scared, must of, because they commenced straining and squawking. They got partly loose and such a wing-flopping you never saw, feathers shooting out ever which way. Made that filly so nervous-wild that she hove up on her hind legs and came down and then kicked up on the front ones, and I couldn't do a thing but sail right over her head and land in amongst all that water and rock. My geese I let go of, in mid-air somewheres, and they sailed off on another track, honking their heads off. That filly give one more rear and tore out like a streak of greased lightning down that creek, and there I lay in the muddy waters. My right arm had hit across a dead tree limb, and by the time I got myself up and started hobbling down towards home that wrist was a-swelling up big as a goose egg and was sore as a boil. It was crooked, too, and so I knew it was out of place or broke.

'When I got home Mam made a great to-do, and said send for this one and that one. The nighest doctor was a day's trip away, by horse, in Hindman, and that arm was hurting me so bad I knew I couldn't stand it that long. Besides, you know a throwed joint ought to be put back into place as soon as ever it can be. The other young uns went to running here and yonder to rassle up some man that would do it, but they soon came stringing back in. It seemed like everybody and his grandpa had gone to Hindman because it was first day of court there. Everybody but Elic, and he didn't want to get near me. He said he hadn't ever had experience with such things, but I begged him so pitiful.

'I says, "Put it back for me, Elic, and stop a-wasting time. I'm a-dying sure. I don't care how you do it but do something. Can't hurt no worse than it's a-hurting now."

'I didn't know what I was talking about, though, for he cotch that wrist and arm with his both hands and shet his eyes and just twisted her straight around, without trying to make it bend or give or settle in a natural way. Boys, I bawled out like a wildcat, big strapping chap as I was. I never had anything to hurt me worse before nor since. I got my horse saddled and rode to the mouth of the creek that very evening, took up at Bess Baer's for the night and went on to Hindman next morning. That doctor like to had him a fit. He said, "Balis, who in God's green yearth done that to your arm?" He put a sling around it, and that thing liked to a-*never* healed up. Fact is I still get shooting pains in that arm and me seventy year old now.

'Well, sir, I was the lostest thing for about six weeks. Couldn't work in the fields, nor do much of anything with my arm tied up. Only thing I could do with it was to move it backwards and forwards thisaway, and I says finally to Mam, "Mam, looks like all I'm ever going to be able to do with this limb of mine is to play the fiddle!"

'She got me an old gourd and me and the boys around there pulled hairs out of the old mule's tail and we worked around till we had us a fiddle and a bow. It had a right fair sound, too, and danged if I didn't keep right on until I had learnt to play "Shady Grove" and a lot more tunes on it, favoring my arm. Then my wrist got so I could take that handkerchief from off it, and soon I was playing for the dancing. They'd say, "Balis, Sal said for me to tell you we aim to run some sets tonight at the stir-off. Bring your bucket and your fiddle!" '

Of Balis Ritchie and Abigail Hall, my parents, their courting and marrying.

OFTENTIMES WE would pester Dad to tell us about how he had met up with Mom, and how they had courted and so on. Children are so curious about such things. But he would never want to talk about that to us, and always told us to hush — it wasn't none of our business. He wouldn't get mad when we asked him, but just acted like it shamed him, and he would look sideways at Mom and give a little dry laugh and go out and study the weather.

It was the evening of their golden wedding anniversary that we finally got all the facts out of Mom and Dad. A soft June evening. The whole community had been in and out of our place that day, paying honor to them. We had cooked for weeks to be able to accommodate everybody with chicken and dumplings with all the trimmings, and it sure had been a big day. All the people brought presents, too. Dad had several gold tie-clasps and watch-chains, Mom had golden hair-combs, earrings, and all kinds of jewelry, and ther were stacks of gold-trimmed trays, dishes, flower vases, and knickknacks, all over the place. Best of all her presents Mom loved the one she got from Dad — a gold wedding band. After all these years!

'I reckon that settles it. I'm really married,' she said.

Finally toward evening everybody went home, and we were resting ourselves with hot tea around the table. Dad had gone off to take a nap after the hard day. The ring must have given Mom nerve, for after a while she went off into their room and came back with the letter.

'I want all you children to see your Pa's letter,' she smiled. 'It's his first one he ever wrote to me. Handle it careful, it's old and crackly. Hard to read, too, yellow and fady, but you can tell what a pretty hand to write he was then. See how even the strokes of it, and the lovely curlicues! He was allus the best scribe in the countryside about, anybody will tell you that.'

Dwarf, Kentucky
June the 23, 93

Miss Abigail Hall
Viper, Ky.

Unknown Friend,

     A friend of yours, Miss Sallie Hall, says that you said you wanted some pretty boy to write to you. I guess you was just joking if you said that to Sallie, but nevertheless I take the liberty of addressing you, asking you to pardon me for my boldness.

     You need not think I am good looking by me writing, for I am not.

     Some of the boys has told me you are a nice pretty girl and of course I would love to see you, for I think we could be friends, don't you?

I will give you a brief description of myself so you may judge what I look like.

I am a young man 23 years of age, height 5 ft. 10 in. weight 1.50 # fair complexion black eyes light hair and stoop shouldered.

If you axcept me as a correspondent I Think we could have some real good fun writing to each other, and very likely our correspondence would lead to something more serious.

There is nothing that gives me more pleasure than receiving nice letters from the girls except being honored with the company of the writer.

I have several correspondents who are strangers to me but we are interested in each others letters and if you answer this favorable I think I can interest you next time. If you should care to see my picture I will send you one with pleasure if you will send me yours. (After I send mine).

Waiting anxiously for a favorable reply,
I remain Your Unknown Friend,
Balis Ritchie
Dwarf, Ky.

Dad came stomping to complain that he couldn't sleep for the noise we were making, and, of course, he saw what it was we were all exclaiming over.

'Abbie, what you a-doing?' He looked sheepish. But we wouldn't hush, and we asked them all manner of questions. Pretty soon they got to having such a good time recollecting that they well forgot we were there in the room.

Mom began musing out loud. 'This'ns the very first love letter I ever got, and then next week he come to see me. Lordie, Balis, do you remember when's the first time you laid eyes on me? It's a pure wonder you would have me after that, but I didn't take to you much neither that first sight we had of one another!

'Pap and all of us were in the field above the house one day in July. It was nigh dinnertime, and we'uz a working hard to get our round hoed out when here come Betton, my baby sister, just a-cutting through the stalks. She couldn't get good breath, she had run so fast. Pap grabbed at her, scared to death. He thought Mam was sick or something.

' "There's a stranger home," she was just grinning and jumping up and down and acting so feisty. "He's the properest thing. Says he's a schoolteacher. From over in Knott he comes."

' "Well what's he wanting here?" Pap wondered. Pap was a good man. He looked off toward the house and fanned himself with his old flop hat. At last he struck his hoe into the ground and started off down the hill. "Dinnertime anyway. Guess maybe I ought to be seeing what he needs of us."

'Betton hollered, "Hunh, he ain't a-wanting to see you. He's come to spark Abbie. He says, 'Does Miss Abigail Hall live here?' " She was a-mocking his voice. "And when I said yes, he lit right down off'n his hoss and come in, said howdy to Mammy Sally, said he guessed he'd wait till Abigail got in home." Betton, she tore out through the corn, and I threw the hoe after her.

' "Hush, you scamp. You don't have to holler so loud and act so crazy. Wait'll I catch up with you, little feisty-britches!"

'Boys, I hated to go in home worse'n I ever hated to do anything. I was the messiest, dirtiest, poorest-looking critter you ever did see. Barefooted, old brown calico dress all tore and faded, old, black, dirty man's-hat with holes in it big enough to throw a cat through. Sweat a-streaming down to my toes, and cornfield dust all over me. And the other girls and Philip 'uz all a-teasing the life out of me cler down the hill, having them a big time. Then to cap it all Mammy Sally run out into the side yard and commenced blowing the living daylights out of the old dinner-horn. Musta blowed it ten or fifteen times fore she run out of breath. Any other time we'd a-thought the house was afire or something, but today I knew it was just her way of teasing me, too.

'Well, I got down to the back gate, and I couldn't stand the thoughts of saying howdy to him and me looking thataway, so I slipped around the backside of the house. Thinks I, I'll just slip in the back room and change my clothes, put on some shoes, and make Betton bring me the washpan back there. Sailed around the corner of the house, and there he was a drying his hands on the towel, and a-grinning like he knew I'd come thataway. Mammy Sally had set him up in the back room to wash and get ready for dinner. Boys, I wisht then I could sink plum through the earth. I wheeled and tuck back around the house. I was so hot and sunburnt and mad that I couldn't see straight. I thought I never would get over it, him a-catching me like that, and him so proper. I stomped into the kitchen, and I just felt like laying them all out east and west.

'Mam whispered, "Well, lassie, wait till you see what a proper man has come to see you!"

'I was about to bust out crying then, and I hollered, "I've done and seen him! Mary-Ann or Rhodie can have him for all I care too. I think he's the ugliest thing I ever saw in my life and I'm not going to pay attention to him."

'So I just washed my face and hands and that's all. Come to the table barefooted and in my ragged dress. Couldn't think of a solitary thing to say to that feller. He kept looking at me and grinning, and I kept on looking at the vittles on my plate. Mammy Sally and Pap and t'others seemed like they had a good time talking to him and listening to him tell, but I couldn't open my mouth to save me. It's a pure wonder he ever looked at me again.

'He come back to see me though. Kept right on till we got so we could talk to one another, and somewhere in during that year we got to talking about marrying. So, we 'uz promised. I was sixteen and him twenty-three. That winter he had to study for his teaching certificate, and couldn't come over much, and then, too, it was a long trip through the mountains from Knott County in the winter weather. In wintertime at home we generally had school for a few months, and I went steady that year. He seemed so much smarter than me!

'I was in what you'd call about the sixth or seventh grade nowadays, somewhere along there. But it was a hard matter to keep my mind on book learning, so it didn't make much difference to me what grade I was in. I'd set with my eyes on the snowy hills and dream about my wedding day. What it would be like, how long off and how close up it seemed, and what kind of cloth Pap would bring me for my dress. To this day I can't work sums with fractions because my mind just wasn't on the lessons that year. 'Pears like I *wanted* to study and learn, but I couldn't somehow, to do any good.

'About the only thing I did learn that whole winter was, I remember, one day some of us girls were a-walking together at recess and Mary Jane Combs got to singing at a little song. Foolish little thing, but I got struck on the words and that evening I walked home with her and made her sing it over until I learnt it. After that I sung it around the house so much that Mammy Sally threatened to whup me if I didn't hush. It was "Somebody." '

1. Some - body's tall and hand-some, Some-body's fond and true,

Some-body's hair is very black and Some-body's eyes are, too. 2. I

Somebody's tall and handsome,
    Somebody's fond and true,
Somebody's hair is very black and
    Somebody's eyes are, too.

I love somebody fondly,
    I love somebody true,
I love somebody with all of my heart

And somebody loves me too.

Somebody came to see me,
　　Somebody came last night;
Somebody ask me to be his bride
　　Of course I said all right.

I am somebody's darling,
　　I am somebody's pride,
And the day is not far distance
　　When I'll be somebody's bride.

Somebody's tall and handsome,
　　Somebody's fond and true,
Somebody's hair is very dark,
　　Somebody's eyes are, too.

'That's pretty. I remember it well, mighty well,' said Dad. 'Seems like I heard it, "Somebody's eyes are blue," though.' Dad has brown eyes.

Mom looked flustered at that, and dropped her eyes to her lap. You could hardly hear what she said when she spoke. She was all smiling. 'It is supposed to be thataway. But I changed it a little,' she said. We all stayed quiet and by and by she remembered some more.

'On the day we got married I rose up before day and crossed over the river down yonder at the shoal to where the rhododendron was blooming there at the foot of the mountain. Seems like it always did grow the tallest and bloom the biggest whitest blossoms right there. I had got a notion to carry flowers at my wedding, and I had been spying on the rhododendron for several days. I gathered my arms full of them and waded back over and started to getting ready. I had to iron my dress, taking care not to scorch it, it was so white. Dad got the goods at the store. It was thin white goods with little ribs in it — now I forget what we called it — and I made the dress myself, in the pattern they made dresses then, with long puff sleeves and a high neck and full gathered skirt.

'The morning passed away so quick, and before I knew it Balis was there, and we were standing up together in the yard, getting married. Uncle Ira Combs married us — I asked for him special. Dad had on a new suit, and I thought I was sure getting a pretty man. They combed my hair high and fastened it with combs, and carrying the flowers made me feel pretty and fine.

'The old custom is to stay the first night at *her* father's house, have a party and the wedding breakfast and so on, then to go the next day to *his* father's house, for the infare. I remember we got up early that first morning of our married life, and we saddled the horses before the rooster crowed and were on the way to Clear Creek before the sun rose. That's thirty mile easy. See if you catch folks today setting out to ride thirty mile one day's trip on a nag! Only way we had though, and it was a high good day we had for going. The sun was shining and it was right warm and windy. My traveling dress was black sateen with white collar and cuffs, and I wore that and rode side-saddle. That was a funny time, that trip. Doc Ritchie they call him now, Sam his name is, he took a notion to go along with us to the infare, and he's allus a right jokey kind of feller. Going across the Duane Mountain he got to showing off what a good rider he was, turned himself around right backards on the old mare and went whooping and hollering, making that nag just gallop along. Come to a bunch of cattle lying in the road, and he says, "Watch me ride right through them cows and not touch a one!" He rode in amongst them, but he couldn't see so well, him setting backards, and as he was twisting around trying to keep the mare from stepping on a cow, a little black yearling raised up right quick just as the horse went over it. Hit the horse in the belly and she reared and Sam went flying off on his head. Didn't have a thing to catch onto, the way he was sitting. Swear we liked to died laughing at him, soon as we found out he wasn't hurt much.

'Well, we pulled in about dinnertime, and they's all waiting for us. I reckon all of Clear Creek was there to see us ride in, and to take our infare with us. The dinner was sitting on the table ready. Chicken and dumplings and turkey and dressing, fresh-killed pork, squirrel, cakes and pies and garden truck. We all sat down to eat and we didn't get up from that table till near dark, and then as I recollect it we wound up with dancing and gaming and singing all night till clear daybreak. Wasn't that a time!'

Dad broke out laughing with his own memories. 'We'd not been married but a day or two when they took a notion to shivaree us. Lordie mercy, seemed like they'uz a hundred people come in on us, but we got to naming them over after that and it was just about ten or fifteen of the boys and girls around on the Creek. But they were a-meaning business and I guess they'd shore have rid me on a rail, hadn't been for Mam getting so vexed and getting ahead of them.

'We were staying at my Mam's then, Granny Katty's, until we could move out to ourselves. Abbie and Katty had just finished washing the supper dishes. We had been somewheres that day, and had a right late supper. Katty was complaining because it was so dark and she had to burn up so much coal-oil to light our supper and their kitchen work afterwards. As I recall, it was one of them black dark nights when you couldn't see hand fore your face, no moon, and clouds kivering the stars up solid. I sot on the porch awhile until I heard them coming out of the kitchen and I got up to go in where they were at, and when my eyes hit that light I commenced batting my eyelids, couldn't see a mortal thing. Little old oil lamp didn't give off much light, you know, but that thick night had really settled in my eyes and even that much light fixed me up so I couldn't see for a minute.

'Whilst I was blinking in the doorway there, the women-folks got awful still and Abbie said, "Katty, do you hear something?"

' "Why yes, I do hear like people whispering and giggling.

I thought it was Balis a-humming to himself but yander he stands on the doorsill."

'Bout that time a man's voice hollered out, loud as a thunderclap, "All right, Balis, come on out now you and Abbie! We come to get you!"

'Didn't take Mam no time to get it sized up. "Them scalawags. They're a-coming in now for to shivaree you young uns. Confound their hides! You'd think they'd be dacent enough to wait a week, anyways. Run, Abbie, you and Balis, you-all can slip out the front way and run off down in the bottom there and hide. I'll tell them rascals you'uns went to Hindman this morning early. Hurry!"

'She pushed the both of us out into the night and shot the door soft, and me and Abbie here lit out down through the bottom, a-stumbling and a-falling along in gyarden truck. By that time my eyes had give it up; I might just as well have been stone blind. Abbie, too. We couldn't see a natural blessed thing, but we finally barked our shins on a log I knew to be close to the road. Behind that log, betwixt it and the palings, was a sort of a sink place with bresh and trees growing round it. We hid in thar and boys, that was a master hiding place. Not too fur away from the house but that we could hear them talk, and with the lamp shining out the doors we could see them all wandering around, all in a puzzlement as to where we had got to. One said he knew we were thar, said he heard Abbie talking to Katty in the kitchen. Katty said he was just teched in the head, hearing booger voices. Her dry, deep voice sounded out plain as day.

' "Sarch about, sarch about, if you won't take my word for it!" she'd say, and she sounded mad. She let out to give them a piece of her mind then, and all the time me and Abbie was killing ourselves laughing out there in the dark.

' "O, now Katty, all we was aiming to do was to catch them home and get you to let us run some sets. Call them out now. Do, Katty. Tell them we won't bother them, just run a set or two, play Boston and Charlie around a little and then go home. What do you say now?"

' "Ef'n you so much as offer to lay a hand on them young uns, I'll make you wish you hadn't. Long as you agree to be civil, though, I reckon you're welcome to stay and pop your heels together some. But only for as long as you stay civil."

'They all give their solemn promise not to do ary thing mean to us, and she stepped out on the porch and hollered us out. They all just whooped and hollered when we come in, and they giggled and joshed us around, made sly remarks to one another for a while. Katty and Abbie flew around setting out candles and lamps and carrying the chairs out into the kitchen. We scrooched the beds back against the wall and in no time atall we were all a-stepping Charlie. Folks passing by in the road heard that good music, and they'd come by in to see why there was dancing at Katty Ritchie's and they not told about it. The ones that came in after the play got sot in its numbers stood around the wall and watched and holp us clap and sing the words.

> Charlie's neat, and Charlie's sweet
> And Charlie he's a dandy,
> Charlie he's the very lad
> That stole my striped candy.

Over the river to feed my sheep
And over the river, Charlie,
Over the river to feed my sheep
And to measure up my barley.

My pretty little pink, I once did think
I never could do without you,
Since I lost all hopes of you
I care very little about you.

Over the river to feed my sheep
And over the river, Charlie,
Over the river to feed my sheep
And to measure up my barley.

Don't want your wheat, don't want your cheat,
And neither do I want your barley,
But I'll take a little of the best you got
To bake a cake for Charlie.

Over the river to feed my sheep
And over the river, Charlie,
Over the river to feed my sheep
And to measure up my barley.

'Well, 'peared like the longer we gamed, the more folks
we gyarnered in. And Granny Katty, she begun to get into
the sperrit of things — she allus did love merriment — and she
fotch out her gingerbread stackcake that she had baked for
Sunday. After I begged her awhile, she even let us drink a
little bit of the elderberry wine that I had holpen her make, and
she got to feeling better and better. Now, if there was anything
your Granny Katty was hard against, it was making a fool
out of yourself over likker, so she was keeping a lookout wherever a knot of boys gathered up to see that no corn was circulating. Once when she was passing by the only window in

the house — they didn't have many windows to speak of back then, just a little hole about a foot square, face high in the hall betwixt the front room and the kitchen — well she passed by and she thought she heard some chaps talking out thar, so she peeped out, and sure enough, there in under the pear tree was four or five of them speaking lowly amongst themselves. Granny knew by the way they acted that they were up to something, so she strained her ears and she heard them a-making it up to "git Balis out and fix him up proper." Meaning to ride me on a rail, and Lord knows what else.

'Granny Katty she just sailed in to the kitchen fireplace, and grabbed her up a shovel full of firecoals, run to that window, reared back, and let them red-hot cinders fly right at the middle of that knot of boys. She was a-letting fly with her tongue, too, and wasn't nobody alive could do that better'n her.

' "YOU low-down villifying varmints! Ain't got the sense you'uz born with! Git from here and don't go showing your face-and-eyes on my place another time this night, ary one of you! Scannle and shame!"

'Boys, them fellers never knew what hit them. They yipped and bellered and lit out in all directions, knocking the firecoals out of their hair. Thar were fellers a-leaping the palings all around the house thar for a few minutes.

'Then Granny and the rest of us had the best laugh about it. They all got the p'int that Katty meant no foolery, though. She made it plain that she had something worse to do to the next bunch that got to sneaking about under pear trees and scheming meanness. Then someone yelled:

' "O, the Devil take the pear tree! Les all go to Boston! Circle up!"

'That was the last of the shivareeing that night. Abbie and me they made be the head couple, and there were so many people scrouged into that circle that it got midnight on us fore we finished up with Boston.

> Good-bye girls I'm goin to Boston,
> Good-bye girls I'm goin to Boston,

Good-bye girls I'm goin to Boston,
Ear-lye in the morning.

Saddle up girls and les go with em,
Saddle up girls and les go with em,
Saddle up girls and les go with em
Ear-lye in the morning.

Out of the way, you'll get run over,
Out of the way, you'll get run over,
Out of the way, you'll get run over
Ear-lye in the morning.

Rights and lefts will make it better,
Rights and lefts will make it better,
Rights and lefts will make it better
Ear-lye in the morning.

Strong dance beat; not too fast

1. Good-bye, girls, I'm goin' to Bos - ton; good - bye, girls, I'm

goin' to Bos-ton; good - bye, girls, I'm goin' to Bos - ton,

CHORUS (sung when extra time needed)

ear-lye in the morn - in! Won't we look pret-ty in the

ball - room? Won't we look pret - ty in the ball - room?

Won't we look pret-ty in the ball-room ear-lye in the morn - in'?

Won't we look pretty in the ballroom?
Won't we look pretty in the ballroom?
Won't we look pretty in the ballroom
Ear-lye in the morning?

Swing your partner all the way to Boston,
Swing your partner all the way to Boston,
Swing your partner all the way to Boston
Ear-lye in the morning.

Johnnie, Johnnie, goin to tell your Pappy,
Johnnie, Johnnie, goin to tell your Pappy,
Johnnie, Johnnie, goin to tell your Pappy
Ear-lye in the morning.

Won't we look pretty in the ballroom?
Won't we look pretty in the ballroom?
Won't we look pretty in the ballroom
Ear-lye in the morning?

'I well remember one song was sung that night. You know how at plays they'll all drap down on the floor when they're given out with the games, and begin to sing, one after another? Well, when they asked John S. Combs to sing, he sung one that had for a long time been a favorite of mine, and I learnt it all out from him, after that. Fore he started his song, he said he aimed to sing a pretty love song, since he reckoned that would be most to mine and Abbie's liking right now. That made everybody laugh and all the girls to turn rosy in the face. You know what song it is I'm talking about; that one that starts out, "I've been a foreign lander full seven long years or more."

I've been a foreign lander, full seven long
years and more;
Among the bold commanders, where the
thundering cannons roar.

I've conquered all my enemies, both all on
land and sea;

I've been a for-eign land-er full seven long years and more, A-mong the bold com-mand-ers where the thunder-ing can-nons roar. I've con-quered all my ene-mies, both all on land and sea, it is my dearest du - el, your beauty has conquered me.

It is my dearest duel, your beauty has
conquered me.

If I should build a ship my love, without the
wood of tree,
That ship would burst asunder if I prove false
to thee.
If ever I prove false my love, the elements
will turn,
The fire will freeze to ice, my love, the sea
will rage and burn.

Don't you remember Queen Ellen, all in
her flowery reign,
As she walked out of her paradise, to cleanse
the golden chain?
Her beauty and behavior, none with her could
compare,

But you, my dearest darling, are more
    divinely fair.

I wish I was a turtledove, just fluttering
    from my nest;
I'd sing so clear in the morning, with the
    dew all on my breast;
So sweetly would be the music, so doleful
    and sad the tune,
I'd sing so clear in the morning in the
    beautiful month of June.

I wish I was ten thousand mile, all on
    some lonesome shore,
Or among the rocky mountains, where the
    wild beasts howl and roar.
The lark, the lilly owl, the eagle, and
    the little swallow too,
I would give them all, my dearest love, if I
    was married to you.

'Lordie now, ain't it quare how things will come back to you so plain like that! I hain't thought of that shivaree night in many a long year now, and still and all it's like it just now happened. Fifty year ago, fifty year, little doney-gal. What do you think of that?

'Thirteen out of fourteen young uns all raised up grown, all good girls and boys, all turned out like we hoped they would, and better, only none of the girls growed to be as pretty as their ma, and I guess I'm better-looking than any of the boys!

'I recollect now even to the end of that there party. Granny Katty said one more song, or game, whichever we would choose. Well, you know a game can allus outlast a song, don't matter how many verses a song has. We'uz all feeling lovey anyhow after all the sweet singing, so we played a kissing game, and

Granny she j'ined in. Fact of the matter I believe she was the
one that led off "Maria."

> I wonder where Maria's gone,
> I wonder where Maria's gone,
> I wonder where Maria's gone
> > Ear-lye in the morning.

> Guess she's gone where I can't go,
> Guess she's gone where I can't go,
> Guess she's gone where I can't go,
> > Ear-lye in the morning.

> Yonder she comes and howdy-do!
> Yonder she comes and howdy-do!
> Yonder she comes and howdy-do!
> > Take a sweet kiss and pass on through!

'Then they finally all left out, and Katty flaxed about like the
Devil was atter her, blowing out lights east and west to save
waste. Did you think that night — thirteen young uns raised
up grown! Reckon we done our share for this old world, Abbie.
Reckon we ought to be thankful to the good Lord that we're
still alive after fifty years to tell the tale!'

Feeding the family. Of our work together in the corn-fields, and how corn was not enough to live on. Of the strange and wonderful career of our D 1, who always could think of one more scheme to make some money in a genteel way.

T HROUGHOUT ALL his years of moving and building and all his life after, Dad has been first and foremost a farming man. The first thing he and the children did when they got to Viper was to clear some newground on one of the steep hill-sides, grubbing up the roots and rolling down the logs for lumber and firewood, and wrestling with the rocks, which lay thick on all the ground. We always had a mule for plowing just as we and most other families around had one cow to give milk. Dad and the boys plowed up the ground, stumbling around the rocky hillside behind the old mule, and the others of us worked with long-handled hoes. The whole family spent the spring and summer days in the cornfield, and lucky was the girl who got to go down from the field in mid-morning to get dinner for us all.

I began my work in the fields as a water-carrier, but by the time I was ten I was an all-day worker taking my own row with my hoe. I felt mighty important and grown-up those first few days, but then the shine was gone; and it was just a tired back bending over the green rows that had no end, grubby fingers reaching down without the eyes seeing to thin out the hill, leaving the two strongest stalks to grow. It was the clinking sound that came too often of hoes fighting the millions of rocks; Dad's tired swearing at the old mule and Mom's weary fussing at him for it; it was sweat that made you wringing wet and bees and pack saddles that stung because of the sweat; it was the stubborn pride that made you keep up with your own row, even though the pace set by the older workers would almost burst your lungs; it was the heaven in the cool shade at the end of the round, the ecstasy in a gourdful of spring water, the foolery in a snatch of song.

Our singing in the cornfield ran to funny songs. They made us laugh and lifted us back to our hoes in a good humor and not so tired. After a long drink from the gourd, Kitty or Truman would likely begin to hum 'Old Tyler,' the song that isn't actually funny but one that we could never get finished because of laughing, and we'd all sing it. Dad would generally always let us finish the song before he hollered, 'Back to work!'

> Old Tyler was a good old dog,
> We thought he'd treed a coon
> But when we come to find it out
> Old Tyler was a-barking at the moon,
>
>   Lord, Lord,
> Old Tyler was a-barking at the moon.
>
> Old Tyler was a good old dog,
> We thought he'd treed a squirrel
> But when we come to find it out,

Old Tyler was a-barking at the world,
         Lord, Lord,
Old Tyler was a-barking at the world.

Old Tyler started down the road,
He started in a run;
He had not gone but a little bitty piece
When he met Allygainy with a gun,
         Lord, Lord,
When he met Allygainy with a gun.

Now Tyler, you did suck them eggs
And this will be your doom!

Old Tyl - er was a good old dog, We
thought he'd treed a coon, But when we come to
find it out, Old Tyl - er was a - bark - in' at the
moon, Lord, Lord, Old Tyl - er was a-bark-in' at the moon.

He sent a steel ball through his heart
And laid Old Tyler in his tomb,
         Lord, Lord,
And laid Old Tyler in his tomb.

Dreams come easy in the cornfield. In between bee stings my mind would run all over the world. The far-off lands in the geography book — what must they be like? What would it be to go all the way to Massachusetts to school, like Unie? She had come home on her vacation full of plans one summer.

'I wonder whether I ought to get a job in Hazard this summer, or if Whitesburg would be better,' she said the night she came home.

'I got a right job for you, lady,' Dad said. 'You a-going to hoe corn. Ain't no girl of mine going to think she's above working in the field just because she's been to college.'

Some day I'd go, too. I'd study college books, and I'd see the ocean, and I'd ride in cars and trains. I'd have clothes that felt good to your skin, silk and velvet dresses like Unie told about.

'Suppertime, gals and boys!'

'First one to the river!'

'One more day's work and we'll have her out of the first weeds.'

When I was twelve years old, on July thirtieth, we were going down out of the field like this talking. I fell behind the others. I came up on a little rise, and there were two hills of corn growing rank and tall up out of it. I stood between the two hills as in a green doorway. The late evening sun slanted straight against my face. I reached out my hands on both sides and held the rich bursting stalks, feeling them sway and stretch with life.

I wondered whether any other person in the world had ever stood just so and thought these things about stalks of corn. I said aloud, 'I will never forget this time. It is the thirtieth day of July 1935, and I am Jean Ritchie who is twelve years old and is standing among the beautiful green corn.' A lump rose up in my throat, my power to feel things and my eloquence was overpowering to me. I wondered if any other girl twelve years old had ever stood still and captured a moment of time like that, knowing what she was doing, and if that girl had ever made a speech about such a common thing as cornstalks.

All of a sudden I felt a great fear. No one was so alone as I was, no one was so different. I ran in a fever to catch up with the others.

The corn crop we planted in spring, hoed in summer, and gathered in the fall would just make bread for the hungry family and feed the mule, the cow, the twenty or thirty chickens, and the two or three pigs during the winter months. The bread from our corn was good. We would get almost to the bottom of the meal barrel, and then would come an evening to have a corn shelling. Sometimes the family did this alone — there were enough of us to shell a turn for the mill in a few minutes — but more often the Brashear cousins from across the branch and the Engle cousins from up the holler would come in and we'd shell enough for three or four turns ahead.

If the older folks were feeling good they'd let the young folks have a cob-fight after shelling was done so long as the boys threw easy at the girls. And, of course, the sheller of a red or speckled ear of corn got kissed and that was all right. Kissing among cousins was no harm, and it was a game anyway, in plain sight of everybody.

Next day Wilmer would take a sack of the corn and throw it across the mule's back so that half the corn fell on one side and half fell on the other, to balance. Then Wilmer would ride Old Maud down the road three or four miles to the water mill and get the corn ground into the best kind of meal I know of. We used it for corn bread, and for making mush in the iron kettle that hung over the log fire in Mom's and Dad's bedroom. We all loved the mush, especially on a cold snowy night. There was cold sweet milk to go with it, and fresh-churned butter most of the time, and sometimes sugar. Mom was always pleased when we bragged on her mush-making, and she would say it was a good thing we liked it. She would look at Dad when she said that, and he would not answer, or maybe he'd trot-a-little-horsie for whatever baby was in the house, and then he'd sigh and say, 'Aye, something'll turn up I reckon.'

Something would always turn up. Dad could always think

up some way of making money in the nick of time. It was after Patty was born — she was the eighth child — that the Ritchies moved from the poor land on Clear Creek to the town of Hindman, and Dad taught in several schools around there. He had to stop teaching long before I was born, though, because his ears had gone pretty bad and he couldn't hear what a chap said when he stood up to recite.

Dad's eighth-grade education and his years of teaching school started him reading, and he read everything to be had from the almanac to Shakespeare. When his children went to high school it was always hard for them to do their lessons at home at night because Dad would get to their books before they did after supper, and Mom would have to be brought in to make him give them up. Partly through his reading he got ideas of exciting things to do outside the cornfield and the garden. His ventures never turned out to last long or make him rich, but he and the family loved the variety.

I remember the pride we all felt when an official-looking letter would come addressed to *Dr.* B. W. Ritchie. That was when Dad sold eyeglasses, and in those days the greatest thrill possible for me was to see that worn black case opened. Rows and rows of little round shiny glasses, and empty spectacle frames and the telescope Dad let people look through to test their eyesight. The case sat behind the organ in the living room, and one day when no one was around, temptation got too much for me and I sat in the dark corner between the organ and the davenport and opened the case. The little glasses seemed to be all jumbled in the case, so I began to rearrange them neatly, according to size. It took Dad two rainy days to restore order, and about that long for my behind to feel normal again. After that I worshiped the glasses case from afar.

About 1905, before folks around had ever heard of such a thing, Dad, in partnership with his brother Isaac, ordered a talking machine from Sears, Roebuck. The nearest freight office was then in Jackson, Kentucky, and Dad and Uncle Isaac walked the eighty miles to bring the miracle machine home.

The trip took a few days, and on the way they stopped for the night at people's houses, promising to have the strange box perform in return for the night's lodging. The news would spread fast and before long all the people for miles around would gather in. They'd fill up all the chairs in the room, sit on the beds and on the floor and stand in the doorways, their faces awe-struck in the pale, smoky lamplight. That machine could talk and sing plime blank like a natural man!

Before they got home Dad had hit on another one of his many plans for making a little money. The family was particularly hard up then. There were three or four children by that time, and they had lost their cow over a cliff and needed to get another one. Here was a chance to perform an educational service to the local people and make it pay.

Dad was never one to brag about his adventures, and I never knew about this experiment of his until I was home from college one time, and we were sitting around the fire after supper, talking about old times.

'I said good-by to Abbie and the young uns one morning, and started off with the talking machine. My prize record was Whistlin' Rufus singing "Little Lizy Jane," and I had a few more — little rolls that favored an ear of corn like. I'd walk until I came to where there were several houses fairly close together, and I'd gather up the people, and they'd pay a nickel a tune. They were awful skeptical when I would set it up.

' "Some trickery som'ers," they'd say to one another.

' "Now you *know* ain't no little box like that can talk. That man's a pyore fool."

'And they'd watch my mouth to see that it wasn't me a-throwing my voice. Well, I traveled through Hazard, Hindman, and up to the heads of the Little and the Big Branches of Ball Fork. Got so folks would hear I was coming two or three days fore I'd get to a place, and my crowds got larger.

'The big day came when I passed through a sizeable settlement on county election day. Folks get more worked up over their politics than anything else, you know, but they say in that place that the candidates couldn't get much excitement stirred up amongst the crowd around the schoolhouse, because "thar's a man come onto the grounds has got a machine can talk and no person inside, it has a great round horn of silver in front . . ." Yes, that thar horn caused me some trouble, too. Some people thought they had to throw the nickels down into the horn to get the contraption to play, and I had to work half that night to get them out.

'Well, so the men and women voted right quick, not standing on ceremonies, and not even stopping to pass the time of day with the election officers. Then they hustled on out so as not to miss the "Whistlin' Rufus" record. That record must've been played forty-nine times that day. Finally at last, the officers couldn't stand it any longer and they begun to complain because folks wasn't a-paying them much attention — mad, I guess, because they couldn't get out into the excitement — and I had to take the talking machine inside the voting house and play it for the men there to keep the peace. No hot tempers and fighting on those grounds all day. Yes, sir, a little music will sure smooth down a crowd.'

Mallie broke into the talk, laughing, 'He come home with a cow! Made enough money — '

'No, now I didn't make *that* much. Traded *her* for the cow, and fotch the money home. Needed milk more'n canned-up music, anyhow, and, then, I was homesick and didn't want to go no further. Yes, a little money ahead allus comes in handy.'

Mom smiled and started to say something, then smiled again. Whenever she does this three or four times you may know she's going to say something funny when she does get it out. Her eyes twinkled and she bent over the churning of milk she had on the hearth beside her to see if the butter was coming. Finally, she said, churning away hard and fast:

'I was in Hazard t'other day and it seemed like every place had one of them juke boxes. Seems like that's all anyone talks about down there now. They act like it's a brand-new thing. I thought to myself the town folks sure did take a long time to catch onto your Paw's idea.'

Another thing Dad did that surprised people was to buy a small second-hand printing press and set about getting out a weekly newspaper. This was while the Ritchies lived at Hindman, before I was born, but one copy of the paper is still among Dad's treasured belongings at home. The *Weekly Record* was, of course, very local in scope, and it was flavored throughout with Dad's own brand of humor. His opinions cropped out unblushingly in what should have been straight news reporting, but since he wrote and printed the paper entirely by himself, nobody could complain. In fact, the subscribers loved it. Men like Silas Johnson would brag for weeks about getting their names in print, even though there was a sly dig about the lateness of his corn crop due to the fact that he was too lazy to hoe it.

Dad printed other things, too, but the only thing that got saved is one copy of his little booklet of old songs which he named, *Lover's Melodies, A Choice Collection of Old Sentimental Songs Our Grandmothers Sang, and Other Popular Airs.* It sold for ten cents and contained twenty songs, among them, 'Casey Jones,' 'Blue Bells of Scotland,' 'Kitty Wells,' and old Scottish-English ballads like 'Jackaro,' 'The Brown Girl,' 'Sweet Willie,' 'Lonesome Turtledove,' 'The Printer's Bride,' and 'A Foreign Lander.'

Other things Dad tried his hand at included the beginning of an apple orchard, the raising of bees, clerking in a grocery store, making tintypes which he developed in his own darkroom, selling 'products' from house to house, politics (he was elected magistrate for one term), and once he started to tell me about when he ran a moonshine still, but Mom came in and put a stop to it, saying that, 'Such tales are not for your children now, Dad. You hush about them days.'

But these money-making ventures never really took the place of the land. Poor, hilly, and full of rocks it was and always would be, but he loved it because it was Land, and as long as you had the Land, you had a way of life that was good and honest and that no one could take away from you.

I always was afraid that when Dad couldn't go to the fields any more he would be fretful with time on his hands, lost to death without the plowlines in his hands, and the long, long rows of green corn on steep hillsides crying to be hoed. But he has laid down those lines more gracefully than anyone I know. Now at eighty-five he still works in the garden, but he does not drive himself to get it done. He works when and because he feels like it. I'll never forget my surprise when, coming home from boarding school after months of absence, I began to notice the change. Dad was in his seventies then, and after dinner that first day he got up as usual, got a drink of water, walked past the door a few times, humming and looking up at the then untended fields. Soon he sat down at the table and joined in the talking and singing that always ends a meal at home. He wasn't unhappy about the empty cornfields; he just seemed thankful that time had set him free to enjoy the family he had worked so hard to raise.

CHAPTER SEVEN

Granddad Aught and Granny Katty. My Dad's memo-
ries of them — what they thought about and how they
lived, the songs they sang and what they believed in —
all of which in a way became a part of me and my
sisters and brothers.

WHENEVER I used to think Dad was strict, the older girls
would laugh at me.

'Strict on you!' Kitty said one day when I made this com-
plaint. 'You just don't know how easy you've got it. If you
think Dad's hard on you, you ought to have been growing up
when we were. You, why, you and the other younger ones get
by with things we first ones never would've dared to think
about. We had to do harder work and more of it than you'll
ever have to, and we had to finish up anything we started to do,

too, fore we could look away from it.

'We had to mind Mom and Dad to a T, and do exactly what we were told and not talk back. Mom hated most of all for us to sass her, and to sass Dad was just not done. I used to think that God would strike me with lightning if I sassed back to Dad. It was fearsome. But Dad's loosened up on the younger generation now. I guess it was too hard on him to watch so close after the children when he saw what a long job it was going to be! Or maybe he saw that young uns left alone would make out pretty well with their raising, anyway. However it was, you sure are getting spoilt.'

I did not think so. It was still pretty fresh in my mind, and other parts of me too, that not more than a short while back, Dad had worn out six apple-tree switches and one off the rose bush on me. That was the only time he ever really whupped me hard, though. He didn't have to, usually. Just speak to me or look at me and that would let me know I had better do whatever it was I had been told to do. Dad believed that if his children talked back or wouldn't mind him when he spoke, folks would say he was not a good hand to raise his family.

I used to worry about Dad because he was so strict. Those times when he would talk to me, tell me stories, rock me to sleep, and sing to me were so beautiful that I could not understand how he could take such little notice of me at other times, or be what I thought was unreasonable and mean. Dad always claimed that the reason he wasn't more sociable with us was because he couldn't hear what everybody was saying. It wasn't until I was nearly grown that I began to understand other reasons. One evening after work I was talking to Dad in the kitchen, and for the first time he spoke freely about my grandfather Austin, his father, who died long before I was born. I asked him if he and Uncle Joe and Wash and the rest ever sung with Granddaddy Aught like we did with *him*.

'Sing with him!' Dad snorted. 'We didn't do nothing with him, less'n he told us to. We were as afraid of him as of a bear. When *he* said something, *we* knowed to jump. He never whupped us but we knowed to mind him. He was strict. Why I guess I was a full man fore I ever spoke to him without he spoke to me first.

'See, folks was not like nowadays, making over their young uns. So we just never *learnt* to talk to him. He never acted like we's there. O, he'd nuss the baby one on his knee, pat it around a little, but soon's we got big enough to talk he let us alone. If we wanted something from him we'd say to Katty, "Mam, ax Aught to let me borry his knife a minute." Like that.

'I can remember just one time he ever whupped me. I was a little shaver about nine or ten year old, and he sent me to the field to get a sack of corn. Told me to hurry back. Field was a right smart piece from the house, and I got the corn and started back. Had to pass a little branch, and I happened to look down and there was some minners a-swimming in a small-like hole of water. I stopped and went to damming them up. The water'd raise up and almost break over, and just fore the minners'd get away, I'd dam them up again. Seems like it got to be the most important thing to keep them minners in that hole of water, and I got so interested and worked so hard that I cler forgot where I was or anything. All of a sudden they's a little noise behind me and I looked back, and there Aught come a-leaping down the bank with a great long switch. He hollered and give me five or six hard cuts about the legs. Boys, I bellered out like I'uz a dying, and wheeled and grabbed that sack of corn and took down the road so fast I plum left him. But that was the only time . . .'

'Did you like him?' I asked.
'Did we what?' Dad didn't understand.
'Did you like him — look up to him?'
Dad studied awhile, then he said slowly, 'Yes. Yes, we liked him. He just . . . never paid us no attention, that's all. After I got grown I'd talk to him around, and would have talked to him more if it hadn't been for the other young uns. Seems like it'd make them ashamed to see me talking to him, and they'd

say, "Listen to Balis now! He oughta be ashamed, talking to Aught thataway!" It'd plague Joe the worst. I don't reckon Joe ever spoke a word to Aught in his life. Joe'd fight him, though. Once Joe picked up a big rock and aimed it at Aught, but Aught just charged at Joe right fast, and Joe dropped the rock and run. Aught allus got the best of him.

'Of course Aught would speak to *us*, understand, when he wanted us to do something. When he spoke to one of *us* we had to go *right that second* on whatever 'twas he wanted us to do. And some ways I believe my Dad's was the right way to do. I believe in chillern a-minding their parents.'

Dad looked at us and laughed. 'Now, when it was with some of his buddies among the men thar, then he'd talk and laugh. Boys! Just let him and Double-Eye Combs and Katty's daddy Solomon Everidge get together and you'd hear some big laughing and goings-on. Old Sol would talk bad talk for them, and they'd might nigh kill theirselves laughing at him. Or they'd get in a bunch and recollect funny things that happened when they were younger. Once I heard Sol a telling how he'd devil Aught when he come a-courting Katty. He said he told Aught, "You needn't come a-courting around here. Ain't nobody can spark my gal unless he can stand flatfooted and —— "

Mom and Mallie had come in to start supper. Mom rattled the skillets loud, but she was listening. She was shaking all over trying to keep from laughing, but the laugh got out anyway in little pieces around the cracks of her mouth and snorts of air through her nose.

'Now, Balis, you hush. Now! Now, ain't you shamed? And pore old blessed Solomon and Aught in their graves too.'

She talked awful mad, and she looked mad too. All but her eyes. She decided to change the subject as she sifted corn meal into the wooden bread tray.

'Granny Katty, now, she was different. She was a good church member, but she was lively. She'd say, "Whenever you get ninety, you're an old woman and I'm not old. Just eighty-nine today!" She kept saying that every birthday up to the day she died and I reckon she was nigh ninety-six then. Make her so mad if someone'd try to set her straight about it.

'She had a right sharp tongue and didn't care what she said or who she said it to. Wouldn't think a thing of calling the President of the United States a blackgyard if she felt like he was one. First time she saw the chillern playing croquet one Sunday she wondered awful and said, "What is it, Balis, they a-doing with them balls and hammers?" Dad told her it was a game they played and it was called croquet. She watched awhile and then shook her head and sort of spit out the words, "Crokay or bokay. Cyards is cyards, I say — right here on the Sabbath!"

'Oh, she smoked her pipe. But that wasn't anything. Lots good saintly old women do that. Smoking a pipe was the style for old women back then, same as 'tis now for some. And she kept her a bottle of corn likker on her mantelpiece. Called it her tonic and she tuck her tonic regular every morning after breakfast. But nobody ever thought hard of her for that.

'I reckon she loved to go to meetins might near better'n anybody I know of. She was the first charter member of the Old Regular Baptist Church on Clear Creek, and in her old days she'd been in the church longer'n any of the preachers, and I think they'uz all a little afraid of her. She'd just as soon tell a preacher what's what as her own young uns. She just sorter made her some rules of her own as to what was right and wrong and nobody never differed with her.'

Mom paused to be sure Mallie poured the right amount of thick buttermilk into the corn-bread mixture, then she beat it hard with the wooden spoon and went on talking.

'One time she started a song in church on the preacher fore he got through even preaching.' Mom stopped and laughed out loud. Then she went on.

'The meetin was long that day — about four or five hours and about four preachers. This one was the last one and he kept a-saying, like most all of them do, "Now brethern and sistern I'm a-goin to quit. One more thing the Sperrit has give unto me to say unto you and then I'm shore a-goin to quit." Then he'd preach on hot and heavy for another fifteen or twenty minutes. He'd get that p'int expounded and then he'd take his hankcher and wipe off his face, and begin again. "Now I'm sartin-lye a-quittin now. Just one more truth afore the Sperrit leaves me." And he'd go to hollern fit to split the rafters and to — just a-pounding his fists on the table again. Granny after he done that the third or fourth time got too restless to set still any longer and she sung out on, "A Twelvemonth More Has Rolled Around," one of her favorites.' We laughed and Mom half-hummed the song.

> A twelvemonth more has rolled around
> Since we attended on this ground,
> Ten thousand scenes have marked the year
> Since we last met to worship here.

'Her voice was quavery and like to get drownded out by the preacher on the first line, but she got stronger on the second, and then people seed what was happening, and they began to join in. Finally the song leader began to line it out, and everybody was singing so loud you couldn't hear the preacher, so he just give up and said Amen and commenced singing too.

Everbody laughs about it yet on Clear Creek, and they'uz all glad she done it, but nobody else *would* a done it *but* Granny.'

'Hunh!' Dad snorted. 'That was being polite for her. Later on she wouldn't bother to start a song. She'd set up on the front seat and when a preacher'd preached a right smart while, she'd ketch him as he passed by in front of her, a-stomping up and down and a-waving his arms and a-raving, she'd reach out and just yank his britches leg and say in a loud crackly voice, "Hold now, Little Erb. You preached long enough. Folks getting tired!" And the preacher shore knowed to slow down and stop right away or she might come out with something that'd really fix him. Never could tell *what* she'd do.'

Mallie dropped a sizable chunk of ham into the kettle of shucky beans. She said, 'Well, she was hard on the preachers, and on all of us for that matter, when she had a mind to be. I reckon May is the only person she never said a sharp word to. She thought May hung the moon. And May thought the world of Granny, always sending her oranges and dainty things, remembering her birthdays and never neglecting to go see her whenever her and Leon got to these parts. And Granny'd even write to May. I guess not another soul of us, now, has a letter from Granny to show, but May has ten or twelve of them, and that's same as a hundred from anyone else because you know it took Granny a week's painstaking work to write a letter, a tablet sheet on both sides. She didn't know how to write until her boys were school age. They'd come in from school of a night and she'd get them down before the fireplace and practice making her letters, and she got so she could write a passable hand. She treated it like it was a gift, something God had bestowed upon her all unexpected, and she used it in a reverent way. It was a big thing whenever she'd decide to write some. She'd say, "Abbie, fetch my tablet and pencil from their place and let me see if today hain't a purty good time to write on my letter." Then she'd sit and muse all evening before her fire, and maybe get two or three sentences put down. Then she'd say, "Thar. Put her away now, fore I go getting proud. Ain't good for a body to do too much and get too smart."

'Now, I'll have to take back what I said about her never saying a sharp word to May, for I remember one time May did get her a little bit riled. One night when May and Leon were visiting us Granny commenced to tell about her walking trip to Morehead when she was a young-like girl in her teens. First time we could remember her telling all of it, but that night she must've got started right and her memory was specially good, for we all got just lost in her tale. After we all went to bed that night we agreed that someone ought to write it out so we'd not forget it.

'The next evening May got her writing things and didn't tell Granny she aimed to write out her tale, and she asked Granny to tell it over again. Well, 'peared like it peeved her a little to go over the same ground again, but she did start it. Wasn't no time till she caught May writing, and she stopped and would not say another word of it. She was awful mad, "I don't have nary thing to say for you to write about."

'The next day, May says, she was washing the dishes, finishing them up by herself, and she heard Granny's stick. Looked up and there come Granny over to where she was, and her old eyes right shammery with tears. You know, Granny never did cry atall. Proud of it, too. May says she sort of leaned on her stick there in the kitchen and couldn't talk out steady for faltering.

' "Honey, it's been a-plaguing me all the long night and day. I'm a mean, cranky old woman, but if it had a-been ary nother soul but you I wouldn't have cared. I just don't know whatever got into me, talking to you thataway. You that's allus so good and so sweet, allus a-doing things and a-remembering. Putting up with an old useless woman's tedious ways. Now I can't figure why I bucked up about letting you write that thar thing down. I can't talk so purty, but then, Lordie, I know you wouldn't try to make fun of me in no way." Then she just broke down, and cried on May's shoulder awhile. "O Lord, child, if there's the smallest kind of a deed that an old thing like me can do in this world that'll benefit anybody, I ought to do it. Now go get your writing things if you're a mind to have that story." '

I asked Mallie to tell the story, for I couldn't remember having heard it all out myself.

'It was away back when the war was still going on, that was the Civil War,' Mallie began over the clatter of plates I was placing around the table. 'Granny says she was just a little chunk of a gal, sixteen going on seventeen, somewheres around there. Uncle Will, Katty's brother, was arrested for a boyish prank in company with another boy. They decided to take a ride on somebody's mule barebacked. Well, the man that owned that mule, he had some kind of a grudge at Will, anyway, was just laying for some way to do him some ill, so he up and had the boys arrested and sent to Morehead. Horse-thieving's a penitentiary 'fence, you know, and so they sent them all the way to Morehead to the State Pen.

'Old man Solomon, Will's and Katty's dad, was all riled up over it and the whole family was mad about it. Sol decided not to cause any more trouble about the matter, though, said Will was young and could stand to learn a lesson, anyhow. So, amongst them in the family they made up the bail to get Will out so's he could come on home. Then they began to hunt around for someone could be trusted to take the money down to Morehead.

' 'Twouldn't do for his dad to go, it was foolish for a man to try to get through Yankee lines at that time. Then they found out there was a woman around near by fixing to make that same trip down on a mule, journeying down to meet up with her man that had got wounded in the fighting. Katty, she spoke up and said she'd go with this woman and bail Will out. Then Will could get home with her some way. You see, Will was just a young un, not old enough to be a soldier, so they figured out that he could get by all right.

'Course, it was a dangerous thing for Katty, and they like to've not let her go, but that seemed like the only way for Will ever to get free, so Solomon got Katty a new pair of shoes and she put on her best clothes and got up behind that woman on the mule.

'I don't know how long it took them, four or five days or more. The woman'd ride awhile and then Katty awhile, for they found they were too big a load for the old mule, both of them at once. They'd take up nights at whatever house they happened closest to when dark came, and by and by they got to Morehead. The woman said good-by to Katty and hoped her good luck at the Pen, and she rode off to find her man.

'Katty never had been in such a big town as Morehead. There must have been close to a thousand people living there back then. She just had the clothes on her back, and I guess she felt dirty and ashamed of her garb there in among so many town people. I guess she must've been afraid too, a young girl like that all alone in a strange place and men looking at her and saying things to each other. But she kept her head, and she found out by asking folks whereabouts the Pen was. She got there and told the head man she had come to bail her brother out of jail. Well, they had changed the ruling or something since the first word was give out, and they told Katty that bail wouldn't get Will out, he'd have to serve out his time. Six months.

'They asked Katty what she aimed to do. She said she reckoned she'd go home. There were some Southern army officers standing there and they heard her. They asked her if she would deliver a message to an officer named Evartts, he was with some of the army that was stationed right close around home. You see, the Yankee lines that she had to pass through between Morehead and home were just on the home side of Salyersville, but our soldiers had stations on both sides of them. They had managed to build out thataway and to stop up the road; back then it was too wild for anyone to travel long through the hills and ridges. The man said he had tried to get the message through by sending a man through the hills, but the enemy had spies for miles around in the woods where they had the road blocked, and these spies had caught his man.

'Katty said she'd try it, and they wrote out the message and she hid it in her shoe. She struck out in the early morning and commenced walking the long ways home, about a hundred and sixty-odd miles. Lordie mercy, it sure must've been a fearful and tiresome journey, with nary soul to keep you company in the lonely places. Houses and settlements were far apart then, and for miles and miles she wouldn't see a soul. She'd take up away before dark sometimes, whenever she'd come in sight of a cabin where folks were good to her, she'd be afraid to chance going on for fear she'd not find another house, or maybe they wouldn't have room to put her up.

'But she got along pretty well. All that walking had made her feet swell and hurt. She couldn't wear her shoes, so she hid the message in her bosom and carried the shoes in her hand. She'd just put them on for looks whenever she'd pass a house. Then her feet got toughened up after a day or two, and she'd stop every now and then to cool them off in a little branch. Then the shoes started to come apart in places. She hated that the worst thing of the whole trip, she said, for it was the first new pair she had got in three years, and they were the prettiest shoes! So she wore them as little as she could, aiming to make Solomon mend them for her when she got home — if she ever did.

'At last she got to Salyersville, and asked to stay all night at a house. The woman lived there was very nice and kind to her, listened to her story and promised to help her get through. Next morning the woman went with her to the enemy lines and told the Yankee soldiers there to let her through, that she was not a spy, just wanted to get home. The men let her pass without searching her. She went on and thought she had passed all the soldiers, and she was scared because she had put the note back in her shoe again. So as soon as she got well out of sight of them, she sat down and took off her shoes and stuck her feet in the branch to cool, and hid the note in her clothes. All at once two men jumped out of the bushes and asked her name and her business. She said she was Rachel Everidge, Solomon Everidge's girl.

'One of them said, "Evartts! Did you say Evartts?"

'She said her name again, and they asked her if she knew

Evartts, the Rebel officer. She told them no, she had heard of him but she didn't know him or much about him. One of them picked up her shoes.

' "I bet you're a spy for Evartts and I think we're going to search you and see." Katty was so scared, she thought that was the end of her sure, even if they didn't search her well enough to find the note, there was no telling what they might decide to do to her once they laid hands on her. She started to cry, saying she meant nobody any harm, just was a poor tired girl a long ways from home. She hadn't ever been off her home creek before this, and she was so scared, everybody so strange and unfriendly. The other soldier, not the one who wanted to search her, said:

' "Oh, let her go. Can't you see she's telling the truth? You come with me, little lady, I'll see that you come to no harm." And the two men walked on each side of her for some two or three miles, and whenever they'd meet any soldiers they'd not let them hold Katty up. Finally they said good-by and wished her a safe journey on home.

'She dragged along the last two days and finally got back to Hindman, tired to death. It was a marvel in the country round, how Solomon Everidge's girl Katty had got safe to Morehead, and had found the way back again through the enemy lines and all the other many dangers, safe and sound and her only sixteen year old. Solomon and all the others sure were glad to see her, they many of them thought they'd never set eyes on her again.

'Katty said the thing she hated most, her pretty shoes were plum wore out, wasn't any use in even trying to fix them.'

We around the table laughed at that. We sat silent for a while, each fellow remembering Granny Katty in his own mind.

I finally said, 'Did she *really* believe in hants?'

'Sure she did,' Mom answered me. 'All the old superstitions and sayings she knew and she believed all of them. Why, every noise she heard out of the ordinary she could explain as something to do with ghosts. Young folks'd try to tease her out of it and she'd just nod her head and say, "Say on, child. I've seen them and had experience with them and I know what I know." You couldn't answer that argument.'

Mom poured the big kettleful of steaming shucky beans into a bowl. I could taste them already, with garden onions and hot corn bread. The rest of the family gathered in as the delicious smells spread through the house and yard. Patty sliced tomatoes and Mom took up a long dish of bacon with plenty of sop to put on the lettuce, with salt. We gathered around. That supper sure tasted good, and all the Ritchies were born with hearty appetites. There was silence for a few minutes while we let the good tastes soak in.

Then Mom said, 'Well, you can believe what you want to about Granny's notions, but that time her Little Marthe seen the ghost is a mighty curious happening.'

'Yes,' said Dad. 'She never would own that wasn't so.'

'Les see, how was it now?' Mom thought it over to herself a minute. 'They'd started some'ers one evening about the edge of dark, and Granny'd dressed Little Marthe up in a new blue homespun dress and put a brown shawl round her shoulders to keep her warm. They went a piece and Granny sent Little Marthe back to the house to fetch her pipe she'd forgot. When Marthe got back she was all white and out of breath. "I seen somethin Mam," she said. Granny asked her what and Marthe began to cry, she was scared, and said, "It looked like me! I was a-passing that old house nobody lives in and I looked over and they was a little girl standing in the door, had on *my* dress and *my* shawl and she was my size and she looked like me!" Granny asked her if the little girl had said anything, and Little Marthe said, "No, just stood there with some wind a-blowing her dress, a-watching me. And then she motioned her hands like she wanted me to come over to her, but I didn't go. I wanted to go so bad I might near did, like somethin was a-pulling me, but then I got scared bad and awful cold and I wheeled and run on here to you."

'Little Marthe tuck sick and died a few days atter that.

– 90 –

Granny allus said that what the girl saw was a warning of her death.

'And then there was something else about Little Marthe, and her singing. Granny said little Marthe was an awful good hand to sing and she just about sung from morn till night. I've heard Uncle Joe and Dad say, too, that whenever she started to school, the way she'd study of a night, she'd stand up in the fireplace corner and *sing* her lessons out. Put a tune to everything. Well, Granny said one night years atter Little Marthe was dead that there was church and she was walking home by herself when the meetin let out. 'Twas a misty-moonlight night and she could hear faraway little ordinary noises like they were close and big. She got alongside the old graveyard up the creek towards home, and she began to hear the prettiest music away up in the holler. It sounded like Little Marthe's voice singing one of her little sweet songs. Only Granny said it seemed like a whole host of voices mingling in. Marthe was singing a high part-like, just sweet and cler as a whittle-ding. Granny said it was the joy-fullest singing ever was. It passed away high over her head and sailed into the graveyard and there it hushed.'

Dad said, 'And did you ever hear her tell of what she saw the night before her wedding day? She swore to the day she died that hit was so.

'She'd gone to bed early and left a purty good fire in the grate and it soon settled down to a solid bed of live coals that shammered out right red and made the room partways light. Something woke her up sudden-like and she didn't know what, but afterwhile she noticed funny jumping shadders on the loft-beams, and then purty soon a red-hot firecoal sailed over the bed.

'She raised up and looked and they was something bout half as high as the shovel — bout head high with the grate. Not a-making no noise, just hopping around, and every once in a while it'd stop and reach in the grate and come out with a fire-coal, roll it around in its hands awhile and look at her with its two shiny little greeny eyes and then, *flip!* The coal'd come flying at her bed and she'd hear it smack on the floor. Then the little black thing'd jig around some more and then snatch another firecoal.

'She said he'd use his thumb and forefinger and take aim about his eye level and hold it there for a minute and grin right mean at her. And then he'd flip it with his thumb and just *dance* around like he'd done something big. Said he kept that up a long time and her too petrified to do anything but set there and dodge, and all of a sudden he just wasn't there no more. She got up her grit and run into one of the other rooms and finished the night with her sisters. In the morning she got to thinking maybe she'd just dreamt it, and went to see. All round under her bed was little bitty cinders. She got the broom and swept them out and got to studying what it all might mean. She tuck it as a warning that she'd have trouble in her marriage, and they all had a time getting her to go through the wedding that day.

'And they *did* separate, her and Aught, when they were old. Atter all their chillern were raised and married off, Aught and Katty got to fighting every time they got in sight of one another. Couldn't give one another a good word atall, and so they just decided to part. I don't rightly know why it was, but they do say that Granny got puny, and instead of Aught staying home and taking care of her he got so he wanted to make eyes at the women all the time. Granny couldn't stand that, she was so jealous-hearted she couldn't see straight anyways. But they wasn't anything she could do but fuss and rail at him. He was a master man, was Aught.'

I said, 'Do you-all remember how Granny Katty used to sit for hours at a time before the fire with her head bowed into her hand, rubbing her eyes? That used to worry me, why she did that so much. Once I asked her, "Granny, does your head hurt you all the time, that makes you rub your forehead and eyes that way?" She stopped passing her hand like that for a minute, then kindly laughed and said, "Why hit's habit more'n anything else, I guess, honey. Sometimes my head hurts and it helps, and times I got so many things want to be thought over all 'twonce it makes my head swim and rubbing it makes me remember faster 'pears like. And, then it's something to do; I don't move around much elseways." Then she studied about it a while and finally she looked at me and smiled and said, "Don't know for shore why-*all* I do it, but child when you get to be eighty-nine year old you'll set fore the fire and rub your old eyes out, too, and you won't know why . . ."'

Mallie said, 'I don't know why it was that being with Granny always made me feel lonesome. I remember after Aught was dead and gone, she was all by herself in that big old log house and she'd send for me to come and stay with her. We'd sit on the porch until about dusty-dark and then we'd get up and go in by the fire. She kept a few coals of fire in the fireplace all the time, even in hot summer. She'd say to people when they asked her why, she'd say, "Well, 'pears like a leettle fire is a company to a body. You can set and see all manner of things in the embers and you don't get so lonesome. You kindly forget they ain't nobody thar but you."

'Well, we'd set there before the fire and pretty soon Granny'd begin to hum and sing to herself. No, she wasn't what you might call a fine singer. Seemed like she wanted to sing, the worst kind, and she was always trying, but she didn't have much of a voice for it. She'd hear a song she loved and she'd study the tune right then and she'd never forget it after that. I guess she sung with me and learnt me more songs than anybody. After she'd hum around awhile she'd say, "Well, les sing a new song tonight." She'd pick out one that I didn't know but that she did, and she'd line out a line and then sing it through and then I'd join in. And she'd never quit one till I'd learnt to sing it by heart all alone.

'Sometimes she couldn't think of one that I didn't know, so she'd hunt in her old songbook and get one she didn't know, herself, and hum around until she'd light on a tune that'd suit it and we'd sing it just as if we'd sung it all our lives. Sometimes she'd make up a brand new tune and say, "That goes pretty well, now, don't it?" Then she'd laugh at herself a little.

'I get to thinking back on them times with Granny and I see that the lonesomeness was mor'n just missing the other young uns at home. Then I was little and hadn't been out anywheres, and I can remember it was like something sort of wondering and sort of crying inside of me and I didn't know what it was made me feel like that, nor nothing to do for it. But just think now, that little tiny girl 'bout eight years old and that old white-headed woman with her cob pipe and her little coals of fire a-setting way out in a big barn of a log house miles from any neighbors, a-singing them old lonesome songs and the frogs a-hollering and no light but a little old coal-oil lamp — Don't that sound like a lonesome feeling time to you?'

Uncle Jason recollects the Ritchie pioneers and names them back seven generations, being especially taken with Great-great-grandfather Crockett Ritchie, who loved fun and music more than anything, and who was a mighty singer of all the old family songs he remembered from his childhood in England.

IN MY high-school days at home, I found my family history much more of an interest to my mind than the book history we had to study. To think about the Ritchie men and women and their children of not many years back roaming the greenwood in Old England, or walking the streets of London Town, would make me chill all over with excitement. I would follow anyone around all day if he would talk to me about old times. I longed more than anything else to go see Uncle Jason Ritchie over on the Big Branch of Ball — that was the Ball Fork of Troublesome Creek. I wanted to go there because every time I'd get to asking questions about those long-gone things, whoever I was pestering would say, sooner or later, 'You know who you ought to meet up with? Nobody but Jason Ritchie over on Ball. He's your own blood kin and it's a sight what all he's collected up in his mind about the family. Reckon he knows all they is to know about this Ritchie generation of yours.'

But Ball Fork was in Knott County, a long way off, and I had to stay home and go to school, because when I was in the seventh grade and already sprouting wings to leave home, we got a high school in Viper. So I got knocked out of going off to the Hindman Settlement School in Knott County by just two years. It nearly broke my heart. Sometimes I'd get to go with Mom and Dad when they went to Clear Creek for meeting and to visit around among all our people over there, but we never did see Uncle Jason. I asked Mom what he was like, and all about him, and why he never did come to see us.

'Well, Jason is your Pa's first cousin so he's not really your uncle, first of all. Just that everybody calls him that; it seems to suit him. If you ever get up on Ball to see him, he'll be dressed up in a black suit, setting back like he's a-waiting for Sunday, don't matter what day it is. He made a lawyer out of himself, and so I don't reckon he ever did a lick of honest work with his hands, but then that's not anything much against him.

'He practiced law all of his life, and once they elected him County Attorney of Knott County, so he always stayed at Hindman to see after his business, though him and his wife had a big farm on Ball. They raised sheep and a right smart of cattle, and besides that they had big gardens and tended corn. Well, Jason, he turned out to be pretty much of a town man, but he'd go back to Ball at meeting times and to see his family. I heard him tell about helping to bury old man Crockett Ritchie, your great-great granddaddy, over on Clear Creek, and he fusses yet that no fitten monument was ever raised over his grave.

'He knows all the old songs, and stories, and will set for hours on end with anyone who likes to listen. That's his best liking.

Sometime, next time I see him, I'll get him to promise to come over and stay a week with us, when the girls are home.'

But the months went by and Jason never did come. I begged Mom or Dad to go over there with me, but seemed like they never had time. They said I couldn't go by myself because it was too dangerous up all those long dark hollers, just a young girl by herself.

Then, one day toward the end of that school year, my English teacher assigned my class to write a long paper about our own lives, an autobiography. I decided to put as much family history into this as I could. I began to write down scraps of information from Mom and Dad, and I'd try to drop remarks that would call to their minds things they had not thought on in years. Then I got hold of a little paper that Uncle Joe Ritchie had started about the family, and when I put all these bits together it made a fairly long paper that I was right proud of. But still I wasn't satisfied, for I knew in my mind that Uncle Jason had much to add to it. I determined to go, alone, to see him.

So, one Saturday I told Mom I was going to Hazard, and I kept right on going on the bus until I got to the mouth of Trace Fork, and I walked the five or six miles across the mountains to where Jason lived on Ball Fork of Troublesome Creek. You had to turn off the Ball Fork road, which was fit for a good-sized wagon, and go a little ways up Beech Fork, where you could only ride a horse through, or walk. The road wound through the deep woods, sometimes a small footpath around a bank, more often going through the very bed of the branch. Ancient beeches, oaks, and feather-leaved walnuts and maples pushed into the edges of the narrow path and locked their branches overhead so closely that I felt I was walking through cool twilight. Only my hot, tingling face and the dust on my shoes reminded me that a bare ten minutes ago I had been suffering the bright mid-day heat of a late summer day.

Suddenly the darkness fell away and I found myself in a clearing. Up on the hillside to my right sat a big house made of great square hand-hewn logs. A porch ran around the front and sides of the house, and a narrow stairway led from the center of this porch to the rooms upstairs. A fence of upright wooden palings marked off the yard, in the side of which sat a tremendous black iron kettle over a smoldering fire. A long neat row of half-gallon jars filled with green beans stood along the ground near the kettle, and other jars waited to be filled when the batch of beans cooking in the kettle should be ready. Off to the left of this spot more palings ran up the hill, forming the enclosure for the barn, the chicken houses, and the smoke house. An old sow and eight or ten little black pigs rooted contentedly in the barnyard, and red and white and speckled chickens strolled about both lots, scratching and making friendly noises. I unlatched the gate and patted the hound dog that came out to meet me, and I saw a tall man with a big mustache sitting leaning back in a straight chair on the porch. He had on a black suit, coat and all, in the summer sun, and he was sitting there with his hands folded in his lap, looking out into the trees. I knew that it was Jason.

'Why, howdy do there,' he said, as I came up the steps. 'Set down here in that chair and let me see who it is you might be.' I told him who I was.

'Shore. I could tell you're a Ritchie, fur as I could see you a-coming, but just which one was a puzzling me a little grain. I guess you're wanting me to sing you a song or two. Your Mammy told me about you. About time you got here; I was getting tired of waiting looking at these old hillsides.'

Uncle Jason's daughter Sarah Patrick came out onto the porch with her little girl. Sarah shook my hand and said dinner was right now on the table, please to come in. Jason waved her away.

'Why Lord, Sary, the kitchen's crowded as 'tis. Now you let this pore girl catch breath after her trip, and you go feed your work hands and your children, and me and Jean we'll have us a talk and we'll eat when you all get done.'

Sarah went back through the front room to the kitchen, and we could hear her putting dinner on the table. Uncle Jason

RITCHIE FAMILY TREE

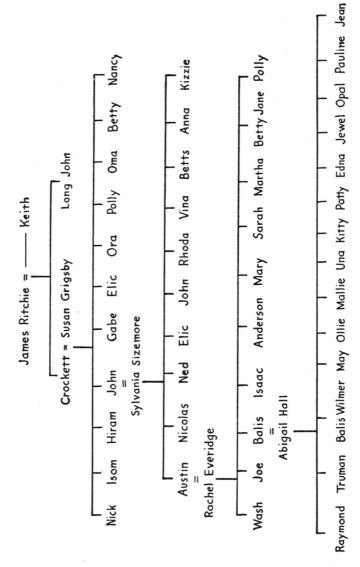

went over to the corner of the porch to the well, drew up a fresh bucket of cold water and handed me a dipperful.

'Set and rest a minute now, and while you're a-cooling off, maybe I can think of a song to sing you.'

I drank deep of the good water while Uncle Jason sat and stared at the topmost mountain ridge across the holler. He began to tap his foot and hum, then to sing softly under his breath, 'Lord Bateman was a noble lord, he thought himself of a high degree,' and by the end of the second verse he was singing out loud and clear on the ballad of the Turkish Lady. Pretty soon I joined in too, for he sang the song with almost the same words and tune we know at home.

Lord Bateman was a noble lord,
He thought himself of a high degree.
He could not rest nor be contented
'Til he had sailed the old salt sea.

O he sailed east and he sailed to the westward,
He sailed all over to the Turkish shore,
There he got caught and put in prison
Never to be released any more.

Now the Turk he had one only daughter
And she was fair as fair could be;
She stole the keys to her father's prison
And declared Lord Bateman she'd set free.

She took him down to the deepest cellar,
She gave him a drink of the strongest wine.
She threw her loving little arms around him,
Saying, O Lord Bateman, if you were mine.

Let's make a vow, let's make a promise,
For seven long years let's make it to stand;
You vow you'll marry no other woman,
I'll vow I'll marry no other man.

Lord Bateman was a nob-le Lord, he thought him-self of a high de-gree, he could not rest nor be con-ten-ted, 'til he had sailed the old salt sea.

They made a vow, they made a promise,
For seven long years they made it to stand;
He vowed he'd marry no other woman,
She vowed she'd marry no other man.

Now seven long years has rolled around,
Seven years and they seem like twenty-nine;
It's she's packed up all of her gay clothing
And declared Lord Bateman she'd go find.

O she sailed east and she sailed to the westward,
She sailed all over to the England shore;
She rode till she came to Lord Bateman's castle
And she summonsed his porter right down to the door.

O, is this not Lord Bateman's castle?
And is his Lordship not within?
O yes, O yes, cried the proud young porter,
He's a just now bringing his new bride in.

Go bid him to send me a slice of bread,
And bid him to send me a drink of wine,
And not to forget the Turkish Lady
Who freed him from his close confine.

What's the news, what's the news, my proud young porter?
What's the news, what's the news, that you brung to me?

There stands a lady outside of your castle
She's the fairest one eye ever did see.

She has got a gold ring on every finger,
And on one finger she has got three,
And enough gay gold all about her middle
As would buy Northumberland of thee.

She bids you to send her a slice of bread,
She bids you to send her a drink of wine,
And not to forget the Turkish Lady
Who freed you from your close confine.

O up then spoke that new bride's mother,
She never was known to speak so free,
O what's to become of my only daughter,
That has just been made a bride to thee?

Well I've done no harm to your only daughter,
And she is the none of the worse for me;
She came to me with a horse and saddle
And she shall go home in coacharee.

Lord Bateman he pounded his fist on the table
And broke it in pieces one, two, three,
Says, I'll forsake all for the Turkish Lady,
She has crossed that old salt sea for me.

When the song was ended, I began to ask Uncle Jason what-all he remembered about our ancestors. I could tell that he was surprised that one of the flighty generation should take an interest in old-time things. He began to smile and clear his throat and look pleased. When I showed him my paper I had started, he said, 'Well, now, what have you got here?' Then he put on his glasses and began to read it out loud, slowly, in his scholarly voice, pausing now and then to fill in with some of his own memories.

James Ritchie with five of his brothers came from England about the year 1768. He settled in Virginia on the James River, while some of his brothers settled in East Tennessee, and the others in what is now North Carolina and Texas. James married a tall, dark-skinned, black-haired woman whose maiden name was Keith. Her father had been killed by Indians just before she was born and she is remembered for her intense hatred of all Redskins.

The story goes that Mr. Keith, his wife, and two children were alone in their cabin when the Indians attacked. Mr. Keith was struck by an arrow and killed, and the woman defended herself and her children with the rifle until at last the attackers fled away. She then lifted her dead husband onto the bed, closed his eyes and folded his hands over his breast and took the children four miles through the Indian-filled forest to the nearest neighbors to get help in laying her man out proper. Her baby was born within the next few days, and it was this child who grew up to marry James Ritchie. Throughout her life, just the mention of the word 'Indian' would send her into a frenzied walking of the floor, her face pale and her body trembling. James fought in the Revolutionary War, and it is known that he was in the Battle of Yorktown where Lord Cornwallis was captured. He told a story about this battle, that before his regiment went into action, the officers had their men to mix whiskey with gunpowder and drink the mixture to make them nervy. It was James' son Crockett who passed this story down to old man Gabe Ritchie. Gabe was at the time of his death the best informed on local history in the mountains. He never forgot anything, and he loved to talk about his ancestors.

Uncle Jason rattled the papers. 'Gabe — yes. He *was* an awful man to remember things. Never had much education and his mind just scribed a little-like circle, nothing else to scrouge it out. What he knew, he *knew*, and it never left him. It was so.' He continued reading.

As Gabe told it, James Ritchie moved to North Carolina in Buncomb County. He pioneered to Kentucky, and died while his family was traveling down Carrs Fork in what is now Perry County, in Eastern Kentucky.

'Yes, now that's right,' Uncle Jason said. 'James and his wife — that Keith woman — they drifted over to Carrs Fork and there wasn't another family there. Virgin timber plum through. Didn't know where they were when James died. Now nobody knows where his grave is. Crockett, he stayed on Carr there and all the rest of the family went back to Virginny.'

Crockett Ritchie, James' son, was the only one of the family to stay on in the Kentucky Mountains after his father's death, the others going back to Virginia. Crockett had his pick of the land on Carr, but it was too lonesome there so he searched around until he found the nearest families, a few scattered ones on Clear Creek in Knott County. At the very head of Clear Creek is some high pretty land in the swag of the mountain, called Hammond's Gap. Now they call it the Gabe Hudson Farm, but Crockett built the first cabin on that land, and married Susan Grigsby, daughter of Bennie Grigsby. To this wedlock were born Nick, Isom, Hiram, John, Elic, and Gabe, sons; and Ora, Poll, Oma, Betty, and Nance, daughters. Poll, Oma, and Nick went to Arkansas and never returned. The remainder of the family stayed in Kentucky.

Uncle Jason rubbed his chin and looked down the branch for a while. He grinned to himself.

'Crockett Ritchie, he was a real man. All the Ritchies around in this country descended from Crockett, I reckon. I remember Crockett telling stories to us children — about playing on the banks of a great river he couldn't see across, and about seeing the British soldiers there, men with red coats on. That was the James River, now, in Virginny. In his prime he was known to be a great hunter. And I have heard people say about him that he wasn't bright — said he wouldn't talk to people much. Just wouldn't take part in their conversation. But as far as I can find out about it, he was way ahead of his time. The ordinary talk amongst folks then was mostly gossip and scandal and it makes me proud that he was above it.

'Fun-loving he was too. Liked parties and plays and helt a many of them. And I guess it was him started us all a-singing. These songs you've got me onto now, they all come from Crockett. Me, I learnt the most of them from old man Will Wooton and he got them from his wife, a Grigsby, and one of the Ritchie girls, and *she* learnt them from Crockett. I guess he knew so many no one ever learnt them all. That old one about Nottamun Town, now, do you know hit? That'n come from Crockett, and hit's might neart sure to be about Nottingham in Old England. Hit goes like this:

In Nottamun Town, not a soul would look up,
Not a soul would look up, not a soul would look down;
Not a soul would look up, not a soul would look down
To show me the way to fair Nottamun Town.

I rode a gray horse that was called a gray mare
With a gray mane and tail, green stripe down her back,
Gray mane and gray tail, green stripe down her back,
There wa'nt a hair on her be-what was coal black.

She stood so still, she threw me to the dirt,
She tore my hide and bruised my shirt,
From saddle to stirrup I mounted again
And on my ten toes I rode over the plain.

Met the King and the Queen and a company more,
A riding behind and a marching before;
Come a stark-nekkid drummer a beating a drum
With his hands in his bosom come marching along.

I bought me a quart to drive gladness away,

. . . .
. . . .

And to stifle the dust, for it rained the whole day.

Slow and smooth, but with movement

In Not-ta-mun Town,— not a soul would look up, not a soul would look up, not a soul would look down, not a soul would look up, not a soul would look down— to show me the way to fair Not-ta-mun Town. 2. I rode a gray on her be what was coal black. 3. She stood so

last ending

drown - ded that nev - er was born.

(Arrangement copyright 1953 by BMI)

When I got to fair Nottamun Town,
Not a soul would look up, not a soul would look down,
Not a soul would look up, not a soul would look down
To show me the way to fair Nottamun Town.

Set down on a hard, hot cold-frozen stone,
Ten thousand stood around me and yet I's alone;

Took my hat in my hands for to keep my head warm,
Ten thousand got drownded that never was born.

'I learnt that one from Will at a play-party, that was the best place to get to learn more songs. When I was growing up that was the place where songs got swapped about the most. For when young folks'd get tired, they'd sit around the fireside and sing for hours on end, or sometimes just until they got their wind back for the games. No, there wasn't much singing all together. Just everybody sang what he knew, all round the circle. They called a lot for funny songs at plays. A favorite one used to be that foolish tale about an old sally buck, another one of Will's songs. You want me to sing that one? Well, let me study hit up.

> I went out a-huntin' sir,
> One cold and winter's day
> When the leaves were bright and sunny
> And the flowers fresh and gay O
> The flowers fresh and gay.
>
> I tracked one sally buck all day
> I tracked him through the snow;
> I tracked him to the waterside
> And under he did go O
> And under he did go.
>
> I loaded up my pistol sir
> And under then I went,
> To kill the fattest buck sir
> It was my whole intent O
> It was my whole intent.
>
> I went down in the waters
> Ten thousand feet or more.
> I fired off my pistol, like

I went out a - hunt - in', sir, one cold and win - ter's day, When the leaves were bright and sun - ny and the flow - ers fresh and gay, O the flow - ers fresh and gay.

A cannon she did roar O
Like a cannon she did roar.

Out of ten and twenty big fat bucks
By chance I did get one.
The rest they raised their bristles up
And at me they did run O
And at me they did run.

My hide it was a-riddled
Till a bulldog it jump through,
And this it made me angry
And my broad sword I drew O
And my broad sword I drew.

I bent my gun in a circle
And I fired her round the hill;
Out of ten and twenty big fat bucks
Ten thousand did I kill O
Ten thousand did I kill.

To the moon I sold my venison,

To the stars I sold my skins.
The man that tells the biggest lies
Commits the greatest sins O
Commits the greatest sins.

'Every time Will Wooton'd sing one I hadn't heard, I'd get around him later on and keep on until I'd learnt it. I got some from other singers, too, and pretty soon folks began asking me to plays just on account of that. I sort of got a reputation for it. But I don't guess that I ever got to be a singer like Crockett to this day.

'He was the most independent man I ever heard tell of, and that led him to do what most people thought was some mighty funny things. One day he told his woman that he was going after a load of wood and was gone seven year. She made inquiries, and it turned out that he and one of the neighbors, a Patrick, had gone to Arkansas. They took their long rifles and walked. Just for the trip. When he got back home he walked into the kitchen and threw down his load of wood behind the stove. Susan said he was a little late with the wood, that the vittles were already done. She tuck up supper for him and the young uns and they set down and eat without ary word said about the seven year in between.

'They got along well, Crockett and Susan. She was a good woman, bore him ten or eleven children. When she died, his children were all married and living to themselves, and he wouldn't go stay with any of them nor let anyone come stay with him. Went right back to their house after the funeral and stayed on there alone.

'In the last year or two of his life his mind wandered. He'd think he had to make the crop like he had when he was young and strong, and in the middle of winter he'd get to worrying about it. Folks'd see him out with a little bucket bout the size of your Mammy's four-pound lard vessel, planting corn in the snow.

'He was about one hundred year old when he died.'

Uncle Jason pushed his glasses into place and read the next paragraph of the family history.

James Ritchie, Crockett's father, had a brother called Long John, who had finally settled on the Crane's Nest in Virginia, and who is known to have distinguished himself during the Revolution, especially in the battles of Monmouth and Kings Mountain. He also fought in the battle of Yorktown.

Uncle Jason stopped and thought. But the way he frowned up his face you could tell he was trying hard to remember something.

'Aye. That Long John I don't know anything about, but Crockett had a brother they called Long John too, I guess after his uncle, and *he*, Crockett's brother that is, went back to the Crane's Nest too, and tuck root there.

'I recollect a quare story now. During the Civil War, Long John's daughters peddled in Kentucky. They'd ride their nags in to the store where they traded, not far from the state line, and they got to talking with some nice friendly girls come in to buy and sell there too, and when they got around to exchanging names they found they'uz cousins, daughters of Long John and Crockett Ritchie.

'Well sir, they made a great to-do about each other, and Long John's girls, they invited Crockett's to visit them in Virginny, and they were planning on it in a big way, when come to find out Long John's family was on the Union side, and Crockett's was Rebel. The girls got afraid to go then, but the Virginny Ritchies promised them all kind of security and protection, and kept on after them about it until they did agree to make the trip.

'And I hear they had a big party and nary bit of trouble. They said Long John played "Killy Kranky" on the jew's-harp, master well too, and that he was an awful feller for singing and dancing all kinds of music. "Killy Kranky"? Well now, hit's

a common-like little fooling tune, keeps dodging about in my
head, but I'll get it out in a minute. Someways like this:

Killy Kranky is my song,
Sing and dance it all day long,
From my elbow to my wrist
Then we do the double twist.

    Broke my arm, I broke my arm
    A-swinging pretty Nancy,
    Broke my leg, I broke my leg
    A-dancing Killy Kranky!

Killy Kranky is my song,
Sing and dance it all day long,
From my elbow to my knee,
Now we'll wind the grapevine tree.

    Broke my arm, broke my arm

A-swinging pretty Nancy,
Broke my leg, broke my leg
A-dancing Killy Kranky!

Killy Kranky is my song,
Sing and dance it all day long,
From my elbow to my toe,
How much furder can I go?

Broke my arm, broke my arm
A-swinging pretty Nancy,
Broke my leg, broke my leg
A-dancing Killy Kranky!

'That there was a little bit of a game they played,' Uncle Jason looked at me sideways and gave a sly laugh. 'Wasn't nothing to it much, you know that winding the grapevine is just a good excuse for the young folks to get their arms around each other. It was respectable, though. Aye, well, let's get on with the history paper!'

Crockett's son John married Sylvania Sizemore, a tiny, fair, blue-eyed woman. She was very active, liking especially to swim. She often boasted that she could swim 'as good as ary man.' Her father was Ned Sizemore. A story goes that the last elk killed in the Kentucky mountains went down before the rifle of Ned Sizemore at the mouth of Elks Fork of Lotts Creek, in what is today Knott County. His daughter Sylvania said it weighed nine hundred pounds, and was one of the biggest ever killed in that country. Ned was a great hunter and a crack shot. When he got too old to engage in his favorite sport, he would wear his shot pouch all day as a reminder of happier times.

'Now I've heard a little about Sylvania. Granny Sylv, they called her,' mused Uncle Jason. 'Yes, she was the one that was part Indian, about a fourth. Her father Ned was half, his father Sizemore having married to a full-blooded Indian maiden. So Sylv had a natural right to be a fine swimmer, just as her Pa, Ned, was born to the hunt.'

To the wedlock of John and Sylvania were born Austin, Nicolas, Ned, Elic, and John, sons; and Rhoda, Vina, Betts, Anna, and Kizzie, daughters. John, the father, was slight of build, with dark eyes and hair. Soft-spoken, a good-hearted man, he belonged to the Old Regular Baptist Church as did most of the other Ritchies at that time. His grandson Balis, Austin's son, remembers that John always wore a long homespun shirt, belted at the waist with a wide woven band, and that 'he never had much to say.' He had such a good turn that he could never deny anyone anything. Folks around would borrow all his farming tools and hunting gear, and if they didn't bring them back, he would never ask for them. Granny Sylv would have to go fetch them back. If someone did something everybody said was a wrong thing, and they'd happen to have conversation with John Ritchie about it, he'd say that it wasn't any business of his; folks that did things like that must have their own reasons. He was so sweet and gentle that Balis remembers him almost with reverence, as though he might have been a saint.

'Yes,' agreed Uncle Jason, 'now, John was your Pa's grand-daddy and my uncle. Elic was my Pap. Yes, Uncle John I remember, and he was just like your Pap Balis says here, quiet and say-nothingy. And yet he didn't seem to be above conversation like Crockett was, too smart for his time, but John, seems like he was more timid, afraid of hurting someone's feelings all the time. Everybody around was in agreement that he was the best soul in the world. Never nobody had anything against him.

'Quare now, ain't it, that Aught was a son of his? All the folks always said how could Aught turn out like he did, wild and restless and rambling. As much different from John as the day is to the darkness, and yet they were father and son. Now, what's next here?'

Austin (Aught) Ritchie married Rachel Everidge, daughter of Solomon Everidge, who lived at Forks-of-Troublesome (now Hindman). Solomon was instrumental in getting the Hindman Settlement School located there. Rachel was a beauty; tall, slender, possessed of dark curly hair and piercing black eyes. She had a fiery tongue that made people wary of her, and a big heart and a dry humor which made them love her too. Her nickname, 'Katty,' bestowed upon her by her father Solomon when she was a little girl, stuck with her, and she was addressed as 'Aunt Katty,' or 'Granny Katty,' until her death at the age of ninety-six, in the year of 1940. The Clear Creek Baptist Church boasts her as its first charter member.

To Austin and Rachel Ritchie were born Wash, Joe, Balis, Isaac, and Anderson, sons; and Mary, Sarah, Martha, Betty Jane, and Polly, daughters.

Balis Ritchie married Abigail Hall, daughter of John Hall of Viper in Perry County. They lived for a while on Clear Creek in Knott County, then moved to Hindman. Just before their fourteenth child was born, the family moved to Viper, Kentucky, where they are living today.

The following children were born to Balis and Abigail Ritchie: Raymond, Truman, and Wilmer, sons; and May, Ollie, Mallie, Una, Kitty, Patty, Edna, Jewel and Opal (twins), Pauline, and Jean, daughters.

'There, young un, I'll be blessed if you hain't got a right complete little paper. History, history, hit's human, hain't it? Like that old newspaper write-up someone copied out about the forming of this county here. That's right uncommon interesting because it talks about some of our people. Wait a minute and I'll fetch and read it out to you.'

He pushed forward and the straight chair which he had been tilting back against the wall logs came down on the floor boards with a thump. He went up the dark stairs that led from the porch to the second floor, and I heard him rustling about among his things; a door screaked, a chest-lid fell shut, and then soon he was back down with a crackly folded paper in his hand. The following account had been carefully copied onto the yellow pages:

From the LOUISVILLE COMMERCIAL for
July 8, 1885, as follows:

The traveler south from Catlettsburg, on the Chatteroi Railroad, will find that the cars stop at Richardson, on the Big Sandy River. In the winter some sort of boat can be secured to Prestonsburg, in Floyd County, but at this season part of the distance must be traveled in a vehicle, which may be described as an ambulance, and part on horseback. Here the traveler is still forty-two miles from the Forks-of-Troublesome indicated by the Act as the seat of government for the new county. Another horse must be procured for the ride over the rough road which follows Beaver Creek for the greater part of the way. Upon arriving at the Forks-of-Troublesome, nothing appears but two or three log houses, not grouped together with any view of making the beginning of a town while vast forests extend in every direction. A road extends to Whitesburg, the county seat of Letcher; another to Hazard, in Perry County, and a third to Jackson in Breathitt. Two of these counties, at least, have made a reputation for outlawry that has extended beyond the State.

On Monday, July 7, 1884, the commissioners named to form the new county . . . assembled at the 'Forks.' The event had been duly advertised through those parts of Breathitt, Floyd, Perry, and Letcher Counties which were to be embraced in the new Knott County. A few persons from a distance were lodged in the 'double' log house, which served as the only inn in that section. It consisted of two log pens, covered by one roof, with a space between them large enough for another room. The second largest

house was the store. The third house was what was face-
tiously known in the moonshine districts as a 'bonded ware-
house.' No distillery was in sight but a plentiful supply of
white native whiskey was served from the log cabin with
the high-sounding name.

Early in the day the neighboring people — and not
all of them near neighbors — began to assemble. The
young people predominated, because a 'good time' was
promised. Rustic maidens accompanied by their swains
and rugged farmers with their families came on foot or
on horseback according to the distance. Soon two fiddlers
of local repute made an appearance, which was a signal
for clearing a small level place near the store, which was
used for dancing through the day. The 'bonded ware-
house' was the chief attraction, however, and the pure
mountain licquor as the good people deemed it, flowed
steadily from morning till night.

With some, numerous potations proved an incentive
for greater agility on the dancing ground — not that anybody was drunk, but 'they war a drinking some.' The
ladies drank more sparingly than their lords, of the white
whiskey, so that none of them, except one or two of
dubious reputations, became intoxicated. The effect upon
the others was to make them boisterous, singing and
shouting, now and then firing a pistol to add to the general
'hilarity.' The People of these counties are the most hos-
pitable in the world, and the most amiable toward strangers
who give no grounds for suspicion. Everything was good-
natured, therefore, though a few small disputes had to be
settled by personal encounters in which no weapons were
employed.

A marked figure in this scene was old man Everidge —

'Now, that there was your great-granddaddy Solomon
Everidge,' Uncle Jason interrupted himself, 'and he at that
time had been a widder-man for about two year, and he was

a-frisking around like that because he was wanting to court Cordelie Combs — you'll take note of her further along in the piece, where it calls her the belle of the ball. That was nobody else but Aunt Cord, as they call her, and then she was the spryest young lass in the counties round. He got her too, and they married, but he died not long after. That's a quare thing about Aunt Cord now, seems like she always married real old men. Just loved to stay by a sickbed and tend to folks. You'd go by and ask her how her man was, and she'd might near always say, "Well, he ain't a-doing no good 'pears like. Right down in the bed and I got to wait on him hand and foot." They say she went on from Solomon and had seven more husbands and outlived them all. Died a widow. In her lone days when she got old she tuck to weaving all manner of baskets, out of willer switches and the like. Got such a big reputation for it that they had her a-teaching the young folks in the Hindman School how to do likewise. The women at the school would make a great fussing over her baskets, say, "Aunt Cord, where'd you get the pattern for this one?" She'd say, "Why honey, hit just come out'n my head some'ers." The women always told her she was a pure artist, and that'd please her awful. She was a good, clever woman. Here, now, let me find my reading place.'

A marked figure in this scene was old man Everidge, evidently at the age of sixty, who had never owned a hat 'cause it made his head too warm.' Nor did he wear any shoes in summer. Not even a coat was needed to complete his costume for the dance. He drank nothing, but was none the less hilarious for that, and danced as regularly as any of the younger bloods. The dancing ground was small, bounded on one side by a dry ditch, which during part of the year is one of the branches of Troublesome Creek. Once while dancing a cotillion, the old man was led to the brink of the ditch by two of these women, whose hands held him, when they suddenly let him go with the effect of landing him on his back in the sand below. It was a great sport for everybody, and the old man lost his temper in consequence.

A figure more noticeable was the belle of the ball — a young woman of twenty, with a most attractive figure and the bearing of a princess. A ruddy complexion, great brown eyes, and a profusion of auburn ringlets were additional attractions. Dressed tastefully she would have attracted wide admiration on any of our fashionable streets. Perhaps she would have excited greater curiosity, however, in her native habiliments. She wore a dress of red calico, severely plain with the exception of a yellow ruffle around the bottom of the skirt, and a narrow blue ribbon about the waist. A small green sunbonnet which did not half hide her ringlets, formed the rest of her attire. The belle wore shoes without stockings on her arrival, but like the other dancers she placed those against the stone wall which lined one side of the dancing ground. She was heared to say that she 'couldn't dance to do no good with shoes on.'

Meanwhile the commissioners were compelled by the general excitement to adjourn to a farmhouse a half mile down the creek, where their business was transacted. It was not altogether a peaceable meeting. The territory to be formed into the new county embraced the homes of the assessor of Floyd County, the sherriff of Letcher, the coroner of Breathitt, and the surveyor of Perry. The first mentioned, Bolling Hall, was named the head of a committee to divide the county into magisterial districts, but refused to serve, asserting that he would never consent to any arrangement which would deprive him of his former well-paying office, as the formation of the new county would do.

Another work of the commissioners was to arrange for the election of county officers a month later and to order a set of blank books for the county records. The latter have been secured, and the bill for them sent, as the law

requires, to Frankfort, to be paid by the State. The shrewd-
ness of these unsophisticated people is shown in the fact
that while no other new county has expended more than
$1200 for an outfit of record books, the bill sent by Knott
was $2100, an amount which auditor Hewitt refused to
pay until forced by law to do so. Thus it seemed that one
of the first acts of the new county was to raid the State
Treasury for the private benefit of a few citizens.

There is a story told at Frankfort which is apropos: The
late James Davidson, while State treasurer, always doled
out the public moneys grudgingly, as if bestowing private
alms upon undeserving persons. One day the sherriff of
Perry came in to make his settlement with the State. There
were twenty-five 'idiot claims,' which were approved by
the auditor who gave a warrant upon the treasurer for their
payment. Mr. Davidson counted the claims slowly and
aloud, turning as he finished, to the sheriff with the remark, 'Why, Mr. Combs, you must be all idiots up in
Perry County.'

'Pretty near, I guess,' was the reply, 'but we generally
have sense enough to get what's coming to us from the
treasury.'

Uncle Jason and I had a good laugh over the little paper,
and then he said I might take it with me to copy out.

At this minute Sarah came and fetched us for a dinner laid
out on the kitchen table — fried chicken with gravy and dumplings on the side, new beans and corn bread, garden greens and
thick, sweet molasses from last fall's stir-off. After dinner we
returned to the porch and fell to singing some more. He knew
most of the ones I knew, and many that I didn't, like 'The
Unquiet Grave.' 'The Miller and His Sons,' 'Lyttle Musgrave,'
and 'Farewell, Dear Roseannie.' The one about Roseannie
sounded more modern than most of his songs, but he insisted
that it was a very old one, although he didn't know where it
had come from exactly, and he sang it with tears in his eyes as

though it had a special meaning for him.

Farewell, dear Roseannie,
And when shall I no more
Behold your fair face
As I've done here before?
  I'll stand at your window
  Both earlye and late,
  So hard is my fortune
  It troubles me great.

When cruel old parents
Came this for to hear,
They stepped to the window
And bid him away.
  Away with Allymander,
  Away with great speed!
  Roseannie is married
  To the squire indeed.

If dear Roseannie has married,
The girl I adore,
I'll turn to the sea
And I'll come here no more.
  So early next morning
  The ship she set sail,
  And early next morning
  She drew a fresh gale.

And all of the sailors
In the sea they were lost,
Excepting one sailor
On a hogshed was tossed.
  Away to old England
  The news to declare,

Allymander is drownded,
Roseannie's own dear.

When dear Roseannie
Came this for to hear,
She wrung her lily white hands

1. Fare - well, dear Rose An - nie, and when shall I no
more be - hold your fair face as I've done here be -
fore? I'll stand at your wind - ow both
ear - lye and late, so hard is my
fort - une, it troubles me great.

And tore down her hair,
    Crying Cursed cruel parents
    For their cruel ties!
    For the sake of Allymander,
    Roseannie she dies.

She pulled out her dagger
And pierced her body through,
Roseannie's blood sprinkled
Like an evening dew.

Crying Curse to cruel parents
Wherever they be,
They'll slight their own children
In many a degree.

The fall sunshine began at last to slant into our eyes there on the porch of the log house, and I said that if I were to walk out the five miles to the big road before dark overtook me, I had better go. Uncle Jason was surprised.

'People's getting so they a-living too fast. Now, what sense was it for to come all this way up in here and just stay these few minutes? Ought to stay a week, anyways. Take that long for me to get started singing good. Well, all right, if your Mammy don't know your whereabouts you best go I reckon. Wait about for a second whilst I hunt up my old hat and I'll walk a ways out with you. I've not talked to you enough to see my satisfaction yet.'

I said good-by to his daughter Sarah and her family and we started off down the creek. Uncle Jason went ahead where the road was narrow and when it went into the creek for a way, he showed me the best rocks to step on, the ones that wouldn't rockle and make me lose my stand and fall into the branch. He talked in his slow remembering way about the Ritchie generation, because he knew I was as thoughtful of it as he was.

'Now it may be that I'm prejudiced; maybe I'm one of the low-down ones. But when they have a right chance seems like a Ritchie will come out. They always take to books and apply their minds when they have a right show. Oh, I'm not saying they're perfect — like anyone else when they get old and get mixed up with a family then they kind of give up hope. And tell the truth there wasn't much to hope *for* — much trouble they had because most tried to raise their families the way they themselves were raised. They seem to think that's the only way, that times don't change. But they're of good stock, the best around here. Scottish and English and Irish the Ritchies are, and they're good people.'

We walked on, Uncle Jason talking slow and steady, and we came to the crossroads where two forks of the little branch rolled in together and made one. He stopped and 'lowed that this was the place to say good-by. He promised to come over to see us soon, and then he said, 'Now what song of all the ones I sung you today did you like the best? That one about the Lyttle Musgrave? It is a pretty thing, the language of it, and the dainty music. Reason I asked you is, I aim to sing your best liking to you for a parting.'

Whereupon he stood up very straight, put one hand on my shoulder, and looked away off somewhere into the pale fall sunset and sang that lovely lonesome song. The little branch waters sang along in a sweet dulcimer drone, like its music was made just in tune for the ballad. Uncle Jason's tall, black-clad frame swayed to the quavery ups and downs of the song and his eyes clouded over with memories. He sang the whole song, all twenty-seven verses of it, and I don't have to tell you that I was black dark getting home.

1. One day, one day, one fine holi-*day, as man-y there be in the year, We all went down to the preacher's house some glori-ous words to hear. We all went down to the preacher's house some glori-ous words to hear.

*pronounced, HOLLYday

One day, one day, one fine holiday,
As many there be in the year,
We all went down to the preacher's house
Some glorious words to hear.

Lyttle Musgrave stood by the church house door,
The priest was at private mass,
But he had more mind of the fair women
Than he had for Our Lady's grace.

The first came in was a-clad in green,
The next was a-clad in pall,
And then came in Lord Arnol's wife
She's the fairest one of them all.

She cast an eye on Lyttle Musgrave
As bright as the summer sun,
And then bethought this Lyttle Musgrave,
This lady's heart have I won.

Quoth she, I have loved the Lyttle Musgrave
Full long and many a day.
Quoth he, I have loved you, fair lady,
Yet never one word durst I say.

I have a bower in the Buckelsfordberry,
It's dainty and it's nice,
If you'll go in a thither my Lyttle Musgrave,
You can sleep in my arms all night.

I cannot go in a thither, said Lyttle Musgrave,
I cannot for my life,
For I know by the rings on your fingers
You are Lord Arnol's wife.

But if I am Lord Arnol's wife,
Lord Arnol is not at home;

He has gone to the academie
Some language for to learn.

Quoth he, I thank thee, fair lady,
For this kindness thou showest to me,
And whether it be to my weal or my woe
This night I will lodge with thee.

All this was heard by a lyttle foot page
By his lady's coach as he ran,
Says he, I am my lady's foot page,
I will be Lord Arnol's man.

Then he cast off his hose and shoes
Set down his feet and ran,
And where the bridges were broken down
He smote his breast and swam.

Awake, awake now, Lord Arnol,
As thou art a man of life,
Lyttle Musgrave is in the Buckelsfordberry
Along with your wedded wife.

If this be true, my lyttle foot page,
This thing thou tellest to me,
Then all the land in Buckelsfordberry
I freely will give it to thee.

But if it be a lie, thou lyttle foot page,
This thing thou tellest to me,
On the highest tree in the Buckelsfordberry
Then it's hanged you shall be.

He called up his merry men all,
Come saddle up my steed,
This night I am away to the Buckelsfordberry
For I never had greater need.

Some men whistled and some they sung,

And some of them did say,
Whenever Lord Arnol's horn doth blow,
Away Musgrave away.

I think I hear the noisy cock,
I think I hear the jay,
I think I hear Lord Arnol's horn
Away Musgrave away.

Lie still, lie still, my Lyttle Musgrave,
Lie still with me till morn,
Tis but my father's shepherd boy
A-calling his sheep with his horn.

He hugged her up all in his arms
And soon they fell asleep,
And when they awoke at the early dawn
Lord Arnol stood at their bedfeet.

O it's how do you like my coverlid,
And it's how do you like my sheet?
And it's how do you like my fair lady
That lies in your arms and sleeps?

O I like your handsome coverlid,
Likewise your silken sheet,
But best of all your fair lady
That lies in my arms and sleeps.

Arise, arise now, Lyttle Musgrave,
And dress soon as you can.
It shall not be said in my countree
I killed a naked man.

I cannot arise, said Lyttle Musgrave,
I cannot for my life,
For you have two broadswords by your side
And me with nary a knife.

I have two broadswords by my side,
They both ring sweet and clear,
You take the best, I'll keep the worst,
Let's end the matter here.

O the very first lick Lyttle Musgrave struck
He wounded Lord Arnol sore;
The very first lick Lord Arnol struck
Musgrave lay dead in his gore.

Then up and spoke this fair lady
In bed where as she lay,
Although you are dead, my Lyttle Musgrave,
Yet for your soul I will pray.

Lord Arnol stepped up to the bedside
Whereon these lovers had lain,
He took his sword in his right hand
And split her head in twain.

CHAPTER NINE

I find out exactly how some of our songs first came into the family. How 'Little Devils' was introduced in the cornfield; how the forbidden gourd fiddle kept alive one of our prettiest love songs; and how I go cow hunting and find 'Fair Ellen,' 'The Hangman,' and a lonesome meeting-house tune.

IT WAS always a wonder to me how families living close to one another could sing the same song and sing it so different. Or how one family would sing a song among themselves for years, and their neighbor family never know that song at all. Most curious of all was how one member of a family living in a certain community could have almost a completely different set of songs than his cousins living a few miles away.

Because we Ritchies loved to sing so well, we always listened to people singing songs we didn't know, and we caught many good ones that way. Some we learned from many different folks and without trying to, so when someone asks us, 'Where'd you learn that one?' we just can't say for sure. But with others we can name the very person that sang them to us. Take 'The Little Devils.' My sister May recalls the day that one came into our family. It came in by way of the cornfield.

'We were behind getting the corn laid by that summer,' May told me, 'but that wasn't much unusual; we generally were. And I was always so ashamed for us to be behind. You see, Uncle Frank Engle's field was over on the hillside next to ours, and him and his young uns'd get up there at the crack of dawn and be working their hearts out even before we'd get to our field. And no nonsense out of them either; they'd not look up until dinnertime, and they'd be back at work soon's they got up from the table. Now, Dad has all of his life laid down for half an hour after dinner before going back to work, and so we all piddled around too, and never hurried back to hoeing.

'Uncle Frank's children were jealous of us, I guess, and they teased us and called us slow and lazy. Even when we'd start work same time as them we'd not get near as much done, cause we'd prank around and sing and make jokes and carry on, and hoe maybe four rows while they over there hoed sixteen. Especially when Unie worked with us; she kept us all a-laughing from daylight to dark. Anyway, in the cornfield we'd hoe along and she'd tell us big tales about what she was going to do some day — sail across the waters and go to big schools and things like that — or tell funny stories about things happened at Hindman School, or stop right in the middle of her row and start to acting like she was on a big stage entertaining a crowd of people. All manner of things like that; anything to keep us from working. I used to fuss at her and try to keep them hoeing, but first thing you know I'd be laughing and carrying on with the rest.

'One day, I recollect, Dad couldn't go to the field after dinner. He had to go somewhere, take the cow to the male or something, so he put me in charge of the hoeing and said he hoped we'd finish up the newground by evening. I felt pretty responsible and I determined in my heart that we'd not disappoint Dad.

'We got to the field and begun to hoe, me taking the lower row because I was the fastest, and Ollie and Unie and Raymond were strung out above me. Over in the other field the Engles were just about to the top of their patch too, but they were laying theirs by and we were just getting ours through the first weeds.

'I told the others, "Now, we'll race Uncle Frank and see who gets to holler first." We always used to all send up a shout when the last hill was hoed at the top of the field. And on the last row, Dad'd always say, "Well, children, it's all over but the shouting now, and the good cool river's a waiting!"

'I decided we were going to do the first shouting that day, but pretty soon I begun to see I was getting farther and farther ahead of the others, and I could look back and see by their actions that there was something going on besides straight work amongst them. Unie'd wave her arms and sing something and they'd all laugh hard as they could. Raymond'd just double up; I thought he'd fall over and roll off down the hill he'd get so tickled. I kept hollering at them trying to get them to work, and they paid me as much attention as if I was a fence post. I got madder and madder, and finally I just laid down my hoe and made for them, aiming to get them to work or know the reason why.

'When I got close enough to hear them, Unie was singing them the song about the little devils that she'd learnt from Uncle Jason Ritchie while she was visiting with his girl Sabrina on Ball Fork. I couldn't get a word in edgeways and I couldn't help but listen, and the song *did* strike me so funny that I couldn't do a thing but double up and laugh too. Then we got to joining in on the chorus, and the whistle part, and before we knew it there was a big shouting from the other field and Uncle Frank's folks's corn was laid by! We scattered out quick and got to work on that corn patch, and I wouldn't let them quit without finishing, and I reckon it was plum gray dark when we stacked up our hoes at the top and let out our yell. Must of scared the hoot owls! Anyway, that song has been a favorite of ours ever since, and I can never sing it without thinking about that funny time in the cornfield with the children.'

There was an old man and he lived near Hell,
  (Whistle)
He had a little farm and upon it did dwell,
  Sing heigh O rattle ding day.

O the devil came to him one day at his plow,
  (Whistle)
There's one in your family I have to have now,
  Sing heigh O rattle ding day.

O, it's neither your son nor your daughter I crave,
It's your old scolding wife and it's her I must have.

So he hobst her up all on his back,
And like a bold peddlar went a-packing his pack.

As they drew near the high gates of Hell,
Sing, rake back the coals, boys, and we'll roast her well.

(Arrangement copyright 1953 by BMI)

O, two little devils come a-rattling their chains,
She hauled back her cudgel and knocked out their brains.

Two more little devils peeped over the door,
She hauled back her cudgel, killed ninety-nine more.

Two more little devils peeped over the wall,
Says, Take her back Daddy, or she'll kill us all.

So he hobst her up all on his back,
And like a bold peddlar went a-packing her back.

Here's your old scolding wife and it's her I won't have,
She ain't fit for Heaven, she shant stay in Hell.

O it's seven year going and seven coming back,
She called for the 'baccer she left in the crack.

O the women they are so much better than men,
When they go to Hell they get sent back again!

I guess it was Dad, though, who was the biggest song hunter of us all, besides Uncle Jason. Especially around the time he got his printing press and took a notion to put out his little songbook, *Lover's Melodies*. He used to tell me, 'I'd hear a part of a song, and if I liked it, I'd learn all that feller knew of it, and then I'd travel around amongst the people in the country here and learn one part from one and another from another until I had the whole song.'

One of the prettiest songs he got in this way starts out, 'I was born in old Virginny, to North Caroliny I did go,' which he learned in full from one of the boys he was raised up with, our neighbor John S. Combs in Viper. Dad always did know a part of the song, but some of the way it went he couldn't recollect, so he got John S. to sing it for him. Dad said the song almost got lost before he got there, for John S. wouldn't have known it either if it had been left up to his daddy, Samuel Combs.

Samuel Combs was called Cedarhead because of his great thatch of hair, it was bright red and shot right straight up ever so far and then bushed out on top all around. Now, Cedarhead was a stern and righteous man and a preacher, and it was his everlasting grief and shame that his young boys were growing up to be wild and to be always after fun and frivolity. They loved playing the fiddle and singing ditties, and those boys were natural-born fiddlers, every one, and they loved fiddling mighty near better than they loved eating. Cedarhead saw this and he at last put it against the law for them to play a fiddle any more, and he broke up every one the boys had made.

Well, the boys didn't do a thing but make more instruments, and they hid them in holler logs in the woods. Then they would get the work done, and say, 'I'm going down the road,' and they'd slip off to the woods wherever it was they had their music hid, and fiddle away, and sing.

One evening Cedarhead was out in the yard, and by and by he heard that devil's music come rolling down the mountain, and it was John S. He had got so lost in his tunes out in a near poplar grove that he forgot and let his bow scrape too loud. Cedarhead followed him there and beat him with a big oak limb. Then he smashed up the fiddle, too.

Once, Cedarhead and his boys were clearing some new-ground, and they got to rolling logs. Nearly all the logs had been prized off down the hill, and the old man noticed that they kept surrounding one log, nearly rotten, a main old big one. Finally he gripped his prizing-pole and stepped to that log. 'Boys,' he thundered out, 'what you a-saving this big one for the last? 'Fraid of straining yourselves?' The boys, they looked at one another and came up kind of slow and timid to help prize. They all hove and set, and that big log went leaping down the mountainside.

It was Dad Ritchie who told me the story. This is his description of how it ended: 'Purty soon the fiddles begun to fly ever which way. Strings a-popping, gourds a-busting — must of been eight or ten of the instruments hid away in there. 'Cord-ing to Cedarhead, he personally tore up Hell in the newground that day!

'I don't know, Cedarhead did all he could to stop them, but the boys they found ways of making their music, and after he died some of them got to be the best musicians in these parts. John S. still remembers and sings a many of the old forbidden songs. "Old Virginny" is what he calls a loving song, and is among the finest ones he knows.'

I was born in old Virginny,
To North Carolina I did go;
I fell in love with a pretty fair maiden
And her name I did not know.

Her hair was of some brightsome color,
Her cheeks were of a rosy red,

(Arrangement copyright 1953 by BMI)

And in my heart I loved her dearly
Many a tear for her I shed.

To my heart you are my darling,
At my door you're welcome in;
At my gate I'll meet you my darling,
O if your love I could only win.

When I am asleep I'm a-dreaming about you,
When I'm awake I find no rest,
And every moment seems like an hour
With aching pains all across my breast.

Your mama says that we never will marry,
Your papa says that it never will do;
If you'll have me, my darling girl,
I will run away with you.

I'd ruther be in some dark valley
Where that sun don't never shine,
Than to see you another man's darling
When I know that you should be mine.

When I am dead and in my coffin
And my feet's towards the sun,
Come and sit beside me darling,
Come and think on the way you done.

'Little Devils' and 'Old Virginny' came into the family a long
time before I was born, but when I was growing up we were
still adding to our store. I remember at least two or three songs
that I learned while I was out cow hunting up in the holler
above home, not a very likely place to find a new song!

Our farm is mostly forested hills with here and there a sizable
cleared place, a few acres, grown over with grass and low
bushes. Dad fenced in one whole mountainside — woods, fields,
and all — for a cow pasture. We usually kept one cow, never
over two, to furnish milk for us all. There was about forty or
fifty acres of this pasture land, so cow hunting in the evenings

got to be one of the biggest jobs around our house.

In my time, Wilmer and I would take turns getting the cows home in the evening. There was always a great temptation for me to stop at Aunt Mary Ann Engle's house on the way back. Aunt Mary Ann is my Mom's sister and makes the best egg-butter of anyone in the county. Well, in the cool of the day, twilight time, we'd come down from the pasture, me behind Old Bill and her heifer Billette. She got named that because Kitty was off at Berea College studying French and she came home in the summertime wanting to Frenchify everything in sight. Dad said she was just trying to act proper, but we all liked the name Billette, so we had us a French heifer, the only one in Perry County, I guess.

As long as one of the cows had a new calf, I knew they'd hurry on home by themselves. I'd turn them through the last bars and watch for a while to see if they really meant business about going home, and then I'd take the side road down to the Engles'.

Usually what took me down that way was the sound of lonesome singing coming from their kitchen. Like our kitchen, this was a separate building from the rest of the house, a brown weatherboarded square room built on the tip of a boulder that overhung a cool pine glen where the branch water tinkled. You could stand on a chair and look out the high back window and see little gleams of it, like pure silver, like the sound of it, like buried treasure, down there in the dark place. The spring was down there, and the big black wash kettle, and hundreds of mossy rocks and pine needles, and secrets! Secrets! You could tell by looking that the dark place was full of secrets, all untold to mortal ears, and I could never find them out.

Chapel and Viola, the youngest two girls, would be getting supper in the kitchen, and the smell of hot crusty corn pone and browning taters, sliced and fried golden brown in the bacon skillet, and thick pieces of home-cured ham sweetened the evening air as it swirled to me on the hill above the house. Blue smoke curled up, too, out of the stone chimney, and that told me they were burning oak in the wood stove, with maybe pine kindling. Mixed in with the sound of supper plates being rattled into place up and down the long eating table was the ka-*pound*, ka-*pound* of the wooden dasher in the churn. That meant for sure a big round bowl of fresh soft butter for the hot bread, and plenty of buttermilk. And there was the sound of the lonesome singing:

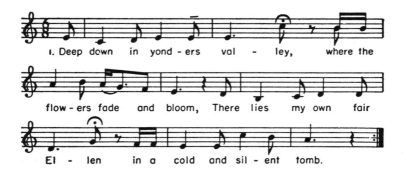

1. Deep down in yond-ers val - ley, where the flow-ers fade and bloom, There lies my own fair El - len in a cold and sil - ent tomb.

Deep down in yonder's valley
Where the flowers fade and bloom,
There lies my own Fair Ellen
In a cold and silent tomb.

She died not brokenhearted,
Nor of disease she fell,
But in one instant parted
From the home she loved so well.

One night when the moon shone brightly
And the stars were shining too,
Up to her cottage window
Her jealous lover drew.

Fair Ellen, let us wander
Down in yon meadow so gay;

While wandring, let us ponder
And name our wedding day.

So to the woods he led her,
His own truelove so fair,
Says she, It's for you only
That I am a-wandering here.

The night is cold and dreary
And I'm afraid to stay,
And I am growing weary
And would like to retrace my way.

Retrace your way, no, never,
Fair Ellen, you must die,
For in these woods I have loved you
And from me you cannot fly.

Down on her knees before him
She begged him for her life,
O Willie, I have loved you
And would like to become your wife.

The birds sung in the morning
But lonesome was their song,
And strangers found her body
In cold and lifeless form.

Farewell, dear friends and parents,
You never will see me no more;
Long, long you'll wait my coming
At my old cottage door.

Come all you fair young ladies
Who chance to look this way,
Don't place your trust in young men
For they surely will lead you astray.

The Engles loved to sing for people. Even a barefooted little cow hunter was treated just the same as if she were a large important crowd of people at a fair. Only no crowd, large or not, ever got such accommodations as I got in Aunt Mary Ann's kitchen. Chapel and Viola would set me down by the table with a sliver of steamy hot corn bread and butter and a dish of Aunt Mary Ann's eggbutter and then act out 'Hangman, Slack Up Your Rope.' Chapel would play the part of the highwayman of the scaffold, and Viola the parts in turn of the father, mother, sister, brother, and, finally, the sweetheart. The last verses were so thrilling that even the eggbutter I forgot:

1. Dear boy I have brought you sil - ver, Dear
boy I have brought you gold, and I have not walked these
long, long miles to see you on the hang - ing pole.

Dear boy, I have brought you silver,
Dear boy, I have brought you gold,
And I have not walked these long long miles
To see you on the hanging pole.

She walked up to the scaffold
And she untied my hands,
She threw her arms around my neck,
Saying, I love this highwayman!

Sometimes, Mom would have to send Wilmer after me with a lantern, I'd forget myself so. On the way home down the dark holler Wilmer'd mutter and threaten what Mom would do to me when we got in home, staying out thataway, but I didn't listen to him much. I'd be thinking about the highwayman and his truelove, thinking how the Engles' way of singing about them seemed so smooth and new, and our way was more old-fashioned and not much tune, sort of like speaking out the lines. I think that even then, I liked our singing of it the better, and I'd sing the words in my mind to keep from dreading so much the whupping I was pretty sure to get at home.

1. Hang-man, hang - man, slack up your rope, O, slack it for a - while. I looked down yon - der and I seen Paw comin' he's walked for a many long mile.

Hangman, hangman, slack up your rope,
O slack it for a while;
I looked down yonder and I seen Paw coming
He's walked for a many long mile.

O Paw, say Paw, have you brung me any gold?
Any gold to pay my fee?
Or have you walked these many long miles
To see me on the hanging tree?

No son, no son, ain't brung you no gold,
No gold for to pay your fee,
And I have walked these many long miles
To see you on the hanging tree.

Hangman, hangman, slack up your rope
O slack it for a while;

I looked down yonder and seen Maw a-coming,
She's walked for a many long mile.

O Maw, say Maw, have you brung me any gold,
Any gold for to pay my fee?
Or have you walked these many long miles
To see me on the hanging tree?

No son, no son, ain't brung you no gold,
No gold for to pay your fee,
And I have walked these many long miles
To see you on the hanging tree.

Hangman, hangman, slack up your rope,
O slack it for a while;
I looked down yonder and seen my truelove coming,
She's walked for a many long mile.

O Love, Truelove, have you brung me any gold,
Any gold for to pay my fee?
Or have you walked these many long miles
To see me on the hanging tree?

Yes Love, O Love, I have brung you some gold,
Gold for to pay your fee,
And it's I have come for to take you home
So you can marry me.

One evening it was my time to get the cows and they were
nowhere to be found. I hunted in all the usual places, but I
couldn't see a sign or a cow, nor hear a bell, so I knew they
must have broken through the fence rails somewhere. Finally,
I found the break. It was a corner where Uncle Lee Brashear's
pasture joined ours and the rails were down in such a way that
the stock in both pastures could have got out through the
same hole, if they had a mind to. Sure enough, while I was
studying the broken fence, up the hill came my cousin Sallie

Brashear, looking for their cows. We figured they must have gone clear over the mountain, so we struck out through the woods together to find them.

We got to talking about everything in the world, and kept on going over the ridges, not noticing how late it was nor how far from home we'd come. The sunlight faded; the birds were singing their night songs in every bush and tree, and the air had a chill snap in it. We clambered over tree roots and through blackberry thickets, and tore our bare legs on the sawbriers, but it was too late to turn back. It couldn't be much farther to the top of the mountain. We climbed, and climbed, and finally panted to the top just as the ghostly-bright blue of the sky faded and it was gray dark, with only one pale point of a star.

The birds stopped singing and the night wind began to sweep silently up from the valleys. We looked for the lights of Aunt Mary Ann's house, but the valley was dark as pitch. There was no pasture fence on top of this hill. We were lost!

We weren't much scared because we knew we couldn't be far from home, only the dark made things look unfamiliar. We stood laughing breathlessly, two little girls not yet in their teens, daring each other to be afraid. Our whispering voices sounded so in the silence that when we'd hush the stillness would ring in our heads. Then the singing began — clear and high and true.

> Father get ready when He calls you
> Father get ready when He calls you
> Father get ready when He calls you
> To sit on the throne with Jesus.

> Away up in Heaven,
> Away up in Heaven,
> Father get ready when He calls you
> To sit on the throne with Jesus.

Strictly and briskly

Father get ready when he calls you, Father get ready when he calls you, Father get read-y when he calls you to sit on the throne with Jes us. A - way up in heav-en, A - way up in heav-en.

Mother get ready when He calls you
Mother get ready when He calls you
Mother get ready when He calls you
To sit on the throne with Jesus.

    Away up in Heaven,
    Away up in Heaven,
    Mother get ready when He calls you
    To sit on the throne with Jesus.

This world is a trouble and sorrow,
World is a trouble and sorrow,
This world is a trouble and sorrow
The only bright light is Jesus.

    Away up in Heaven,
    Away up in Heaven,
    This world is a trouble and sorrow
    The only bright light is Jesus.

We'll all be happy in the morning

We'll all be happy in the morning
We'll all be happy in the morning
A-sitting on the throne with Jesus.

Away up in Heaven,
Away up in Heaven,
We'll all be happy in the morning
A-sitting on the throne with Jesus.

The wind did strange things with the old modal melody. Its cadences rose and fell over the solemn hills with unbelievable beauty. I could have believed without much persuasion that it was a host of angels. Granny Katty's superstitions came over my mind and I was swept back in time. This could be a visitation of angels warning me of my father's or mother's death; it might be our guardian angels sent by the Lord to guide us home; I may have died and was just entering Heaven . . .

Sallie broke in on my trance. 'It's Hez!' she whispered, 'Hez Kilburn and his grandchildren. We're just across the branch from Hez's. We missed the pasture by coming too far around the hill before we crossed.'

'Hezzie Kilburn. Whoever heard him *sing?*'

For years Hez had gone up and down the branch by our house, carrying corn and flour, hauling wood. He was silent for the most part, unsmiling, civil but not overfriendly, and always seeming to be deep in thought. His shy, flaxen-haired granddaughter Cory sometimes sang old songs in school programs, but nobody thought to ask her where she had learned them. Nobody thought of her at all, because she was little and quiet and her big blue eyes had the look of a hunted rabbit. She and her little brother Willie dressed sort of shabby and they lived in an old shack that was falling down and it was rumored around that the county had to help support them. Whoever would have thought that Old Hez could sing like that?

When we were almost down to the cabin, the singing stopped.

'Let's go in a while,' I said.

'I've never been in there,' Sallie hung back. 'Some say they've got an awful bad biting dog.'

The rickety door stood open at the top of a long flight of plank steps blackened with the weather and rotting around the edges. A single coal-oil lamp burned with a soft light that made the place, with its gray bare boards and little furniture, seem cheerful. Old Hezzie was sitting in a straight chair leaning forward in an earnest way. He was near blind and was looking closely at a little black book — the *Sweet Songster* that the preachers sang from in Mom's church. Little Willie sat on the floor beside him, chin in his two hands.

'Ne' mind, now,' Hezzie was saying, 'ye didn't 'member it all that time, but that's the way ye learn, hain't it? Now here, let's try her again.'

About that time they saw us standing on the steps, and, after staring at us hard for a minute, Hez asked us if somebody was sick at the house, then if we were lost. Willie ran into the kitchen and set out two more chairs for us. They both seemed very sheepish that we had caught them singing, and wouldn't sing any more. His woman Suze had taken Cory and gone visiting down the line, Hez explained, and Ben, the boy's father, had not come home.

'He hain't to be kept account of since Omy left him. Acts right crazy; wisht he could find him another woman and settle down and do right by his young uns. Willie here is going on seven year old and he sorter gits lonely with an old man like me. We'uz just singing there to sorter bring the night on, so's we could sleep. Didn't think about nobody hearing us.'

Old Hez smiled one of his rare smiles.

We begged them a while longer, and finally they began another song, but they sang in scared voices, almost under the breath. The old man's voice creaked and the little boy's was no longer high and clear. The spell was gone; the magic was back up there on the black hilltop.

CHAPTER TEN

Brightest and Best . . . The Ritchies Take Christmas

I GUESS CHRISTMAS is without a doubt the best time in the whole year, all around the world, for all folks who celebrate it, and in our family in Kentucky it must be better than any place else. I suppose every child must feel that way about his own home place and his family and their Christmases together. I can remember looking forward all year round to the happy time in December when all the scattered ones of us would gather in around our fireplace and sparkling tree. Just thinking about it would fairly send me out of my mind with joy and excitement.

One Christmas is plainer to me than any other. I don't know why it should be, but maybe because it was the year I was eight, and the others were going to take me caroling with them for the first time. Or it might be because that was the year Granny gave me the brown-colored doll.

used to keep the Post Office over on Clear Creek, and she got to read all the papers that came through for folks. Anyway, the stories of how Christmas was celebrated off from here got to Mom, and she decided one year to make a Christmas tree for us. Dad and the others — Uncle Wash and Uncle Isaac and them — they thought it was all foolery and wouldn't be of much help about it, but on the day before Christmas Mom called me to come, her eyes just a-shining and said secret-like, "Put on your coat; I want you to help me do something." I got my coat and ran out with her. I could tell by her way that it was something nice. "What is it now, Ma? Where are we going?" She kept smiling quick little excited smiles and she said, "I want us to go hunt up a Christmas tree!" Gee-oh, I could've tuck wings and flew, as they say, I was so tickled.

'We got us a hatchet and lit out in the worst snowstorm you just about ever saw. We had to fight our way through the deep snow already on the ground, across the branch, and up the steep bank to the road. The nearest evergreens were pretty far up in the hill. It was hard going, slick ice in under the soft snow, and to cap it all it began to snow even harder, the wind slapping it right into our faces. We couldn't see hand before us, and the wind was blowing so hard we couldn't stand. Mom grabbed my hand. "Have to go back," she hollered above the storm noise. Well, I began to cry. I knew if we went back, it'd be too bad to come out again after this storm, and Christmas would pass and no tree.

' "Come *on*, I said!" She sounded mad. Then she said, "I see us a tree we can get to — don't *have* to be a pine now does it?" Down by the branch across from our house were growing some little sycamore saplings, and Mom took the hatchet and cut down one of them. It didn't have any leaves, but the little woolly winter tags were hanging right pretty all through the limbs of it.

'We took that tree home and propped it up in the front room, and that night after supper we decorated it. Let's see, we cut colored paper out of old catalogues and tied them here and there with bright wool threads, and we strung popcorn and hung it around. And the next morning when we got up, there were big apples, saved for winter in the cellarhole, hanging from the branches. Under the tree was a big plate of molasses candy Mom had made.

'As I look back on it now, it was a kind of a quare Christmas tree, but to us all then it was the prettiest thing we'd ever laid eyes on. We just couldn't get away from it. I remember the whole house was full of the good smell of the winesaps. That was the *happiest* Christmas!

'Word got around. Someone came to borrow something, and after dinner here come Wash's girls and more neighbor young uns. They all liked it fine, and I was proud that there were apples enough to go round. Then we all played games around the tree.

'Next Christmas Uncle Wash's folks had a Christmas tree too, and then more families up and down the creek. Now I guess everybody everywhere celebrates the day this way. Almost it seems like there was never any other way. But in the evening on the fifth day of January, I always remember Granny Katty sitting bowed over the fire, singing of the little babe with dewdrops a-shining on His cradle.'

We all began to sing Granny's song, softly so she wouldn't hear us, for we wanted to sing it for a surprise beneath her window in the morning.

Hail the blest morn when the great Mediator
Down from the regions of glory descends,
Shepherds go worship the Babe in the manger,
Lo, for a guard the bright angels attend.

Brightest and best of the suns of the morning,
Dawn on our darkness and lend us thine aid,
Star of the east, the horizon adorning,
Guide where our infant Redeemer is laid.

Not too slowly

Hail the blest morn when the great Med - i - a - tor
Shep-herds go wor - ship the Babe in the mang - er,
Star of the east — the hor - i - zon a - dorn - ing,

Down from the re - gions of glor-y de-scends.
Lo, for a guard the bright ang-els at-tend.
Guide where our in - fant Re -deem-er is laid.

Bright - est and Best of the Suns of the morn - ing,

Down on our dark - ness and lend us Thine aid,

Cold on his cradle the dewdrops are shining,
Low lies His head with the beasts of the stall;
Angels adore Him in slumber reclining,
Maker and monarch and king of us all.

Say, shall we yield Him in costly devotion
Odors of Edom and offerings divine?
Gems from the mountains and pearls from the ocean?
Gold from the forest and myrrh from the mine?

Vainly we offer each ample oblation,
Vainly with gifts would His favor secure.
Richer by far is the heart's adoration,
Dearer to God are the prayers of the poor.

So we talked and recollected and sang the midnight away,
and then we got too drowsy to keep to our thought to stay up

all night. We all stretched out with our clothes on, some of us on pallets before the fire, some across the chairs, some on the beds in the back of the room. The boys all went out to the little room where they slept — Raymond and Truman and Wilmer were all home then — and we got two or three hours' sleep.

Edna and Kitty seemed like the ones who always saw that everybody got up and out for the caroling those cold mornings, so about three o'clock they hollered us all up. We were so sleepy we could hardly live, but we moaned and stretched and gawped and finally got awake enough to know what day it was and what we were doing all piled up that way. We began to say 'Christmas Gift' to each other, and fuss about who said it first to which one. Then we got a good whiff of the coffee Kitty had started in a pot over the fire, and I knew I could have some because it was Christmas. We were in a big hurry, for Kitty wouldn't let us touch a drop of coffee until we got just ready to go out except our very top coats. So the girls raced each other with the clothes, and we had the coffee about drunk up before the three boys dragged in, looking still asleep and mad at being pulled out of their warm beds. When Edna would go to get them up Christmas mornings, they'd generally say, 'Oh, this year I don't think I feel like going. My head hurts me!' But none of them got away with that, and inside of a half-hour we'd be ready to go.

We stepped out into the shivery still morning. The snow was ankle deep and the world was shining like silver. beneath the wispy circle of a moon and the big Christmas star, the 'brightest and best of the suns of the morning.' The old earth was like it was holding its breath and waiting for a holy thing to happen. We went around to Granny's window, keeping very still so as not to waken her too soon, and we sang 'Brightest and Best' for her. Then for Mom and Dad came 'Good Christian Men Rejoice,' and then 'Wondrous Love' that Grandpa Hall loved so well. As we sang, it seemed that thousands of people and a thousand years sang with us the simple words that know no time, that never fail to make me chill and tremble to my heart.

What wondrous love is this
O my soul! O my soul!
What wondrous love is this
O my soul!
What wondrous love is this
That caused the Lord of bliss
To bear the dreadful curse
For my soul?

When I was sinking down
Sinking down, sinking down,

Slowly

What__ won-drous love is this,__ O my soul,__ O my
soul, what won-drous love is this,__ O my soul, What
won-drous love is this, That__ caused the Lord of bliss,To__
bear the dread-ful curse__ for my soul,__ for my soul, To
bear the dread-ful curse __ for my soul?

When I was sinking down
Sinking down,
When I was sinking down

Beneath God's righteous frown,
Christ laid aside His crown
        For my soul!

To God and to the Lamb
        I will sing, I will sing,
To God and to the Lamb
        I will sing!
To God and to the Lamb
Who is the Great I Am,
While millions join the theme,
        I will sing!

Ye winged seraphs fly,
        Bear the news! Bear the news!
Ye winged seraphs fly,
        Bear the news!
Ye winged seraphs fly
Like angels in the sky,
Fill vast eternity
        With the news.

And when from death I'm free
        I'll sing on, I'll sing on,
And when from death I'm free
        I'll sing on;
And when from death I'm free
I'll sing and joyful be,
And through eternity
        I'll sing on!

We went down the branch and up the county road, our
same track as every other Christmas morning. 'Noel' for Aunt
Maggie and Uncle Lee, and 'Silent Night.' Aunt Maggie always
put a lighted candle in the window when she heard us, to let

us know she heard, and to thank us. For Clarindy Hall's folks we sang 'Midnight Clear,' and for our sister Ollie 'Once in Royal David's City' and 'Away in a Manger' because she had so many children and they all liked those songs.

We plowed on up the road, beating our hands together and running now and then between houses to keep ourselves warm. Wilmer carried the lantern and by its light I could blow out a breath and see it like a big steamy cloud between me and the Morning Star, and I would try to make a big enough breath to shut out the Star, but I never could.

'Here's the Campbells' house. Sh-h-h. Grace likes "Holly and Ivy," in the new tune we sing at Pine Mountain. Hope their dog don't bark.'

By the time we had sung our way up to the Post Office — that's where most of the houses in Viper are — it was five o'clock or so, and we began to see a light in a window here and there. It was so late we didn't go to every single house, but we all stood in the road there and sang four or five songs to all the homes ranged around us on the hillsides. Mark Cann's folks were up, and they came out and hollered to us a Merry Christmas and to come on up and warm up before the fire. The children were just getting their presents, and it was a sight to watch them. The Canns gave us apples and nuts and candy and great mugs of hot coffee. Then someone noticed it was getting daylight out, and we all broke in a lope for home to get our own stockings. Some ran the railroad and some the county road, and we all made good time. Running along we could see through everybody's windows hung with holly wreaths, see the little ones in their nightshirts pulling their stockings down from the mantelpiece, taking out dolls and choo-choo trains, candy sticks and oranges, their faces all happy at the same time for once.

Patty halted us all in front of Mrs. Haddix's. The house was still dark and we wondered whether Mrs. Haddix had heard our first carols. So we went in through the gate and bunched around her window and sang a lively one, 'Joy to the World,' to be sure to wake her out of her sleep this time. We hadn't much more'n got the first line out before the top part of the window flew open and we knew she was there listening. We sang on, and she struck a match to light her candle. I could see her hands all trembly. The candle shot its little flame up and shone on her face and hair. She had the prettiest hair, soft and wavy and white as the snow we walked on, and in the light of her candle the white rounding edge of it framed her face in a soft circle and made me think of a white angel. She just stood still there and listened to the song, crying softly to herself. When we finished, she said:

'Oh, God bless you children, and God forgive me for being in doubt of you. I — Lord, I was feeling so bad, I thought you had passed me by this Christmas! Ought to a-known better than that, but I got up so as to be here ready for you, and then I was just sitting here feeling sorry for myself. I want to hug all of you. Sing, sing, now. Sing my "Noel" for me, and don't mind if an old woman cries a little.'

We went on again then, and as we turned up the holler toward home, she was still waving her candle at us and calling, 'Merry Christmas.'

Wilmer and I ran a race to the house to see what was in our stockings. It was a rule in our house that we could look in our stockings first thing Christmas morning, but that we couldn't touch any of the presents on the tree until after the whole family had gathered into our house from their separate homes near by, and dinner was over, and the dishes washed.

As I ran along, I thought of the letter I had written to Santy Claus, a few days back. I had put the letter up the chimney in the girls' bedroom where there was no fire built. I made sure Granny and Mom knew where I had put it, and the next time I went to look, it wasn't there, so I knew it was safe in the hands of Santy Claus. The letter said:

Viper, Kentucky

Dear Santy Please will you bring me a doll and a shoot gun and a flashlight this christmas. Your good friend, Jean Ritchie.

I almost ran my legs off trying to beat Wilmer to the house, but he outdid me and got ahead. I was afraid he would grab my stocking and not let me have it, to tease me, but when we burst in through the door, there before the fire sat Mom and Dad and Granny Katty waiting for us. So Wilmer went straight to his own stocking and didn't even let on that he saw mine.

I stood and studied the looks of my stocking for a minute. It stuck out in a queer way for certain. I took it down and felt all over the outsides of it, wondering if I had got what I had asked for.

Dad said, 'Open it up there, why don't you? Standing there feeling the outsides of a stocking won't tell you what's in it!'

So I pulled out the long peppermint cane sticking out of the top, then I put in my hand and felt something smooth and cold. It was a glass pistol filled with hundreds of red cinnamon drops. Santy had brought the shoot gun! Maybe the other things were in there too. I had about given up hope days ago, for the girls had told me at least a hundred times in the last week that Santy sure would not bring me a thing, I was so mean.

The bottom of the stocking had two round bumps in it, big ones. These would be an apple and an orange, I could smell them already. On top of them would be nuts, hulled-out black walnuts and hickory nuts, hazel nuts from the bushes at the top edge of the newground, and maybe peanuts and the big wonderful English walnuts from the store. Then there'd be a few pieces of hard Christmas candy. All this I knew from past Christmas stockings, but what was in that funny-shaped middle part?

I rammed my hand in and pulled out the thing that was making the stocking poke out sideways. It was a flashlight, and not a play one either, a real one, black and silver-colored, that would burn bright whenever I slid the shiny button up. I put it down quick, like it was hot, and plunked down on the floor the better to get at the stocking. First the shoot gun, then the flashlight, now the last lump must be the doll.

My fingers fastened around her chest and arms and drew her out slowly. She was wrapped up in a red handkerchief that looked like one of Granny's head scarfs. I jerked that off and she lay there naked in my lap. I kept looking at her, batted my eyes several times. A doll all right, but something was wrong about her. The color of her skin was dark brown, all over.

I looked up and Dad and Mom and all the others were gathered around to watch what I would do. It went through my mind all in a flash how the other little girls, Ollie's and Aunt Maggie's and May's, would likely get dolls that day, pink and white baby dolls, lady dolls with real hair, fairy dolls with wings and lacy clothes. They'd ask to see what kind of a doll I got, and I'd have to show them. Then they'd laugh at me and make fun of my doll, ugly little brown thing with one straight black pigtail on its head, and nothing on its body but an old head hankcher. I had the most miserable feeling; I don't know of a time since then when I've felt so ashamed. I thought they were picking on me, even on Christmas Day they couldn't stop teasing me. I kept on just looking down at the doll and I didn't say a word.

Then Granny began to cackle out laughing, and Wilmer pranced all around the room and he whooped and hollered out in a sing-song: 'Jean's got a nigger doll! Jean's got a nigger doll!' Over and over.

'What's the matter, child? Cat got your tongue?' Granny asked me. 'And how do you like your new poppet?'

I couldn't stand it. I yelled out, 'I won't have it! I hate it!' Tears flew all over my face and I threw the doll down hard on the floor and I ran through the closet hall into the girls' room and crawled under one of the beds as far back as I could, and there I lay and snubbed my hurt up into the dusty bedsprings. Granny came in after me. I could see the closet curtain brush to one side, and her apron hem and her high black shoes coming slow out behind it. They stood still while she looked around for me with her dim old eyes.

'Now where've you got to and what ails you anyhow? Swear

if I don't think the pyore devil's in you. Acting like that!'

It was all Granny's fault. I hated her. I stuck my head out and looked at her, and I reckon I must have been scary-looking. My hair was red and wild and my face was wet and streaked with dust and dirt. I was choked up, but I managed to yell out at her. 'Yes, and if I was a devil you know what I'd do? I'd take you by the hair of the head, and I'd drag you all over this room!'

That hit Granny funny and she laughed so hard that she nearly fell over on the floor. I ducked back under the bed. 'Lord God, look at that Ritchie down there!' Granny could not do much good to get her breath. ''Fore my die, I ain't been so well reminded of Aught Ritchie in a coon's age! Guess it ain't your fault how you act, exactly. You come by it honest.'

She finally hushed chuckling, and her apron hem was still. Then her voice said, 'What's the reason you don't like the poppy-doll? Cause it's different from the ones the other young uns got? I wouldn't mind that if I's you, you'll have something not another young un in the whole caboodle of them will have. Hush and don't cry.'

The high black shoes turned at last and shuffled uncertainly back toward the closet. The curtain brushed aside, and then the backs of the shoes stood still again. Granny's voice sounded like she was talking to herself.

'*I* thought it was a purty poppy-doll — hush and don't cry.'

Their voices came through the closet hallway — Granny's laughing, telling what I said about being a devil, Mom's scandalized.

'I'm going right in and pull her outa there and whup her good if it is Christmas Day!' Her chair screaked.

Granny's voice again, raspy and kind, 'Let her be, let her be, Abbie. Hit's just the Ritchie in her coming out. And don't devil her bout the poppy-doll, she'll get over it. I ought to a-knowed better.'

Chairs pushed then and they began to all scatter out and clean up the house and get the dinner. After a while I crept out and went through the hall to the front room, and slipped on back into the big room. I took the brown doll and crawled under the Christmas tree to the corner of the organ. I pushed the organ out from the wall and put the doll behind it and pushed the organ back again. Then Mom hollered for me to go to the well and draw up water enough to get dinner with, and in a few minutes I forgot all about the ugly doll.

Mom said to draw up the water and then carry in the buckets one at a time, because Wilmer and Carol were busy cutting up stove wood for the day. I took the two store water buckets and the big old wooden piggen from their places. What water was in them I put into the teakettle to use in the cooking and washing the dishes. Then I ran out the slippery path to the well.

That day the wellbox looked like it was made out of ice. Where we had drawn water and it had sploshed out as the bucket came over the top, icicles hung down from all the little stick-out rocks the wellbox was made of. They looked good. I broke off many of them and ate them like candy. Then I ranged my buckets round so they'd be easy to get at when the drawing bucket came up, and I took hold of the drawing rope, which was looped over a nail on the side post and was so stiff with ice that it stuck together in the loops and wouldn't hang out straight. Worse than that, the big iron pulley hanging from the cross top pole was all gummed up with ice and the rope stuck in it. I had to climb part way up on the slick rocks of the wellbox and work at the pulley with my hands, pull the rope backward and forward until she finally slid loose. Then I let the cold snaky rope run through my numb hands, and the bucket went zing down and hit the dark far-off waters. It took a minute for the bucket to turn over sideways and slide under, then when I felt the full pull of it I began to draw it out, hand over hand. It was awful hard to keep hold of the rope and it slick as greased lightning with that ice coat on it, and I can tell you that by the time I got all the vessels filled, my two hands had pretty near come off. I couldn't even feel them.

I carried the buckets one by one into the kitchen and Jewel lifted them up on the water shelf for me. Then she sent me off to the fire to thaw out, and I noticed on the way through the big room that the grandfather clock's hands said almost eleven. Time for everybody to start coming in. I warmed a little and then ran to the front window to watch for them, and I was all excited. It is a fine feeling to be watching the road on Christmas Day for good friends to come and play with you. Ollie had four girls and one boy, and they lived down the branch and around the hill. They were all ages around me, the oldest one, Ernestine, not too much older than I was, Helen and Kathleen near my own age, Amanda still little and sweet to play with, and the little boy-baby — 'Brother' we called him — whom we could hold and rock if we were good. We used to have some mighty good times. Ernestine, I had seen this morning when we sang carols, but somehow that seemed like a week ago and I was anxious to see her again.

There they were! Ollie carrying the least one, Raymond carrying Amanda, and Ernestine, Helen, and Kathleen balling along through the snow. They picked their way, slipping and sliding, down the steep little bank to the footlog and edged across it, up through the bottom by Aunt Maggie's house, across a smaller footlog, around the path above the branch, through the sandbar, and then aside to our house. I ran to meet them in the sandbar to yell 'Christmas Gift' and help them carry things. They were loaded down with baskets of food and bright packages to go under the tree, and Ernestine and Helen and Kathleen had their arms full of toys. Christmas mornings when they had their tree they always picked out a few of their new playthings to show off among the other children. Dolls and such things. Ernestine had a tall lady doll with real curls, because Ernestine was always such a lady-like little girl herself. Helen and Kathleen had sweet-faced baby dolls just alike. They had long, long dresses and they cried when you turned them over. I said my doll must be under the tree this year, I had to wait until after dinner to show it off.

We all poured into the house and I watched Ollie and Mom unpack the baskets Ollie's folks had brought. A great big kettle full of chicken ready to cook, apples and bananas and grapes and home-canned cherries for fruit salad, a good-smelling juicy meat-loaf baked in a dishpan, a chocolate cake as big as a mountain. We all stood around, and our mouths were sure watering over all that feasting food. Mom fixed that.

'Swear you can't stir 'em with a stick! Jean, you and Wilmer take all the young uns, now, and go off and play. If it's too cold outside, why go in through the closet hall to the girls' room. They's a good fire there. Don't hang around in the front room around that fire, now, cause that's where Granny and all the menfolks has to sit. Go it! What makes young uns want to stand right in under a body's feet like that for? We'll holler for you when dinner's ready.'

So we played and sang and told tales and chased one another around, until we got so hungry we couldn't keep our minds on play any longer. We began to dart through the hallway into the other room where all the menfolks and Granny Kat sat talking and laughing around the fire, and the brave ones got their heads into the big room where the Christmas tree was. Then we found out that if we slipped in quiet-like and stood still and listened or looked at the tree, and just smelled deep of the air without *saying* how hungry we were, that no one noticed us and made us go back into our room. So little by little we settled down in around the beautiful tree, and it was a sight how that pile of presents had heaped up since the morning. While we were there Edna came slipping in with her arms full of packages that she had just gone and wrapped up in red and white paper, and some were in paper covered all over with little green holly leaves and red berries.

She poured them all down on top of the big stack, and that brought them clear up to the lowest branches. She picked up the ones that fell out too far on the floor and stuck them here and there in among the green branches.

'Jean, have you been feeling of the presents again? Don't you know that if you do that, you won't get a one? Not one lonesome little present stays in under the tree for little girls that squeeze the bundles.' Then she smiled and we all hollered and squealed, because she didn't do a thing but begin reaching and squeezing of them herself!

'We better all get out and away from this tree fore Mommy comes in and whups all of us. I tell you what, come on over here to the organ and I'll sing and teach you a Christmas song I bet you don't know.'

The best place to stand at the organ is on the side, where you can face Edna as she plays it, and you can lean against the organ itself. One side was covered up by the tree, so we all raced to stand on the other side.

'I bet I do know that song,' I said. I couldn't believe there was a Christmas song I didn't know.

'You don't know this one, because the school children have just learned it at Hindman. Miss Payne over there heard the little colored children singing it over at the mouth of Breedings Creek and she taught it to her school children. Some lined up on one side of the room, and the rest on the other, and they sang the parts of it back and forth to one another.'

Moderately

Chil-dren, go where I send thee: How shall I send thee?

Lively

I will send thee one by one 'Cause one was a little bitty ba-by
two by two 2. two was the Paul and Si-las
three by three 3. three was the three wise rid-ers

Wrapped in swad-dlin' cloth-ing, Ly-ing in a man-ger,

Broadly

Born, born ___ O! Born in Beth-a-lye-hem.

Children, go where I send thee;
How shall I send thee?
    I will send thee one by one,
    'Cause one was a little bitty baby
    Wrapped in swaddlin' clothing,
    Lying in a manger.
Born, born O! Born in Betha-lye-hem.

Children, go where I send thee;
How shall I send thee?
    I will send thee two by two,

        'Cause two was the Paul and Silas,
        One was a little bitty baby
        Wrapped in swaddlin' clothing,
        Lying in a manger.
    Born, born O! Born in Betha-lye-hem.

The song built itself up to 'ten was the Ten Commandments,' and by the end of the second or third we had caught onto the pretty tune of it and were all singing right along with Edna. We would have made Edna sing it over again and again, all the way down from ten, only we just couldn't think of a thing but the sounds and smells coming out of the kitchen, right at that particular time.

At last, I said that I was starving to death for a drink of water and I walked bold as you please into the kitchen. But I needn't have been scared, they were all rushing about like hens on a hot rock, and no one even noticed me. Everything was getting done at the same time and they were trying to get dinner on the table while it was good and hot. Dad and our boys, and Roy Estepp and Leon Deschamps, Ollie's and May's men, got called in from their fireplace to carry in the little tables from the cellar and the living room so as to make the eating table long enough for all of us to get around.

You never saw such a bustle, seven or eight women in one little kitchen all cooking their special dishes. Ollie was the chicken-frying expert, and she was turning out dishpans full of it, brown and crispy-crusty. Nobody but Mom could make fitten dumplings, least to hear her tell it, and she was hot and happy over the big black iron pot on the back of the stove. She was so fixed on making those dumplings the best ones she'd ever made that as she went back and forth between the table where she had them rolled out on the doughboard to the pot where she dropped them into the gravy, she trompled on every cat and dog and young un that didn't get out of her way in time. Mallie was watching the oven where a big pone of corn bread and the long square pan full of biscuits were turning a tender gold. May fixed platters of deviled eggs and the wooden bread tray full of green sallit. Pots of nutty, meat-seasoned shucky beans stood already done in the warming closet, together with long pans of hot mealy yellow sweet taters baked in their own skins. Edna spread soft and creamy icing on her yellow butter cake, and mashed up dried apples and spiced them with cloves and sticks of cinnamon to go between the seven layers of Mom's gingerbread stack-cake.

Kitty was busy with a surprise. She stirred and mixed and grinned, kept her recipe book covered over with a towel, kept peeping in under to read what it said to do next. Patty tended to the skillet of fine-cut Irish taters frying in deep bacon fat. When she turned them over they hung together in brown sizzling sheets. Jewel and Pauline were doing the most exciting thing — cutting up all kind of fruits into a big glass bowl. Ripe red apples, canned cherries, peaches, and strawberries from our own cellar, and wondrous things from the store only for Christmas, oranges, tangerines, fat bananas, raisins. Then when all the fruit was cut up, they sliced fluffy white marshmallows and scattered walnut kernels on top.

It seemed like a hundred years until they finally got the last dish on the table and hollered dinner. The other young uns had managed to get into the kitchen, too, one by one, and we just couldn't understand why the menfolks kept hanging back by the fire, waiting for someone else to start and being so polite. I felt so hungry that I had the idea I could eat up every bit of all that loaded-down table full of vittles and still not want to quit.

At last everybody found places, Dad at the head of the long board, Mom at his left-hand side, all the menfolks beside their women and all the children scattered about among their mothers and the other big girls. Then Edna led us in singing grace to God, and looking around that table I think we sure had a lot to be thankful for. We sang a part of the wassail song, changing the words a little to make it suit.

Love and joy come to you,
And to you Merry Christmas too,
And God bless you and send you a Happy New Year,
And God send you a Happy New Year!

Why is it that you can never eat anywheres near as much as you think you can at a feast like that? I always did feel like I'd missed out if I didn't eat some of everything on the table. We children were proud of that among ourselves, as a matter of fact. But I will have to tell on myself that I slid by that day with just a bite or two of ordinary vittles, like corn bread and sallit greens and both kinds of taters, and took my bait on the special holiday things like the fruit salad and the three or four different kinds of cake. The pieces of fried chicken and the helpings of dumplings and gravy were just too many to let on about.

We little ones always loved Christmas dinner because that was one day that nobody cared a hoot if you started out with cake and jam the first thing, and wound up the meal with a chicken leg, or whether you did or did not drink your milk. Of course, the baby ones'd get started off with someone poking into their mouths a mashed-up mess of chicken livers and gravy over crumbled-up biscuit or taters, but pretty soon that babe'd be sitting in under the table with a chicken bone to gnaw, and a piece of butter cake in the other hand to change off on. Just so we weren't crying or showing off, that's all they cared — and we had a fine time.

About the time when we all had begun to push back our chairs and slow down a little bit, in came Kitty with her surprise, grinning away, her face all shining in the light from it — a great plum pudding, blazing and sizzling. Lord, how we all hollered! Then May's and Ollie's men, Leon Deschamps and Roy Estepp, they whispered a minute and then went out and brought in a bottle of sweet red wine. Of course Mom spoke right up and said they'd not be drinking in her house, but Roy said there wasn't enough of it to get drunk on by the time it went the rounds of us all, and he poured out a little bit and made her taste of it first. She tasted and tasted and made a face a time or two over it, and finally she said it didn't taste too strong, and anyway it was Christmas Day, and the most of her children were home.

'Best time of the year to celebrate, guess. Besides, the Bible does say that a little wine for the stomach's sake is for the good.'

Then came the dishes, and such a mountain stack of them you

never did see. Every spoon and paring knife in the house was to be washed, and right away, too, for Mom had learned from past Christmases that if we opened the presents under the tree before the dishes were washed, we'd be night getting them done. Mom just naturally hates to see dishes sit around not washed and put away, so she made a rule that every last dish and pot had to be washed and in its place and the kitchen shining before we got even a smell of the Christmas presents.

It didn't matter how little you were. If you were big enough to handle a drying rag you had a hand in that dish washing, and woe be unto the one that tried to dodge out of it. Of course the old folks and the men and the main cooks didn't have to help — they went into the front room to talk and wait for us. Pauline and Jewel took time-about washing in the big pan on the stove, and we little girls all worked like ants around in between the two big rinsing pans and the cupboard. Every few minutes someone from the other room would come in to say hurry, the tree was about to break down in every limb with so many presents, and it sure couldn't hold out much longer.

I never saw so many dishes in one kitchen in my life before. It seemed that we just never would get done. Some of the littler ones were slipping off from us and not coming back to help finish, hiding off in under a bed somewheres and not answering when we hollered for them to come back. I was thinking of trying the same stunt myself, though I knew for certain *I* could never get away with it, when Jewel said whyn't we all sing a very long song and race to see if we could get done with the dishes before we got done with the song. It was an old trick of ours to make the work go faster.

Pauline struck up then with 'Barbry Ellen,' and I do reckon that's one of the longest songs in the world, and, of course, we put in all the verses we ever did know, so that we would win the race. We didn't rush the tune of it either.

In Scarlet Town where I was born
There was a fair maid dwellin
Made every youth cry well-a-day
And her name was Barbry Ellen.

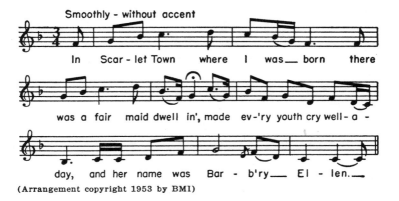

All in the merry month of May
When the green buds they were swellin,
Young William Green on his deathbed lay
For love of Barbry Ellen.

He sent his servant to the town
To her own father's dwellin,
Sayin Master's sick and he bids you to come
If your name be Barbry Ellen.

So slowlye, slowlye, she got up
And slowlye she came nigh him,
And all she said when she got there,
Young man I believe you're dying.

O yes I'm sick and I'm very sick
And I never will be any better,
Until I gain the love of one
The love of Barbry Ellen.

O yes you're sick and you're very sick
And you never will be any better,
For you never will gain the love of one
The love of Barbry Ellen.

O don't you remember in yonders town,
In yonders town a-drinkin?
You drunk the health of the ladies all round,
And you slighted Barbry Ellen.

O yes, I remember in yonders town,
In yonders town a-drinkin;
I gave my health to the ladies all round,
But my heart to Barbry Ellen.

He turned his pale face to the wall,
For death was on him dwellin,
Farewell, farewell you good neighbors all,
Be kind to Barbry Ellen.

As she was going across the field
She heard the death-bells knellin;
And every stroke they seemed to say,
Hard-hearted Barbry Ellen.

As she was going through the woods
She saw the pale corpse comin;
Lay down, lay down that corpse of clay
That I may look upon him.

The more she looked, the more she grieved
At last she burst out a-cryin,
O take him away, O take him away,
For I myself am dyin.

O Mother, O Mother, go make my bed,
Go make it both long and narrow,

Sweet William has died for the love of me,
And I shall die of sorrow.

O Father, O Father, go dig my grave,
Go dig it both long and narrow,
Sweet William has died for me today,
And I'll die for him tomorrow.

O she was buried in the old church-yard,
Sweet William was buried a-nigh her
And out of his grave sprung a red, red rose,
Out of Barbry's grew a greenbriar.

They grew and they grew up the old church tower
Till they couldn't grow any higher,
And there they tied a true-lovers knot,
Red rose around greenbriar.

Well, we sung along on that, and we ran hither and yon like bees in a honeycomb trying to beat that song through. About two verses before the end we saw we had too many dishes still left, just a few too many, and that the song would finish first. We began to sing it even slower, dragging out the tune until you could hardly recognize it, and have time to giggle and laugh between each word. And it the saddest part of the song, too. I remember I felt kind of bad because we were carrying on in such a disrespectful way, and both of them stretched out dying. Then here came Mom through the kitchen door, walking hard on the floor like she meant business. She slapped her hands and hollered to us over the noise.

'Shoo — oo — weee! Lord help my time-a-day, young uns, what's ailing you all in here? All this time over a little dab of dishwashing, and no wonder. Fiddling along with an old slow song like that one. If you are wanting to get anything done quick, you have to sing a fast song. Here, give me that dishrag.'

Dad was following close behind Mom, to find out what was

taking us so long. He joined in the rukus, and began to sort of clog about, stomp, and clap his hands like he was dancing. He never followed doing foolery like that, and it just tickled us all to death to watch him. He began to say out a little old rhyme that I remember he, and Mom too, used to say when they trotted the babes on their knees, about the twelve days of Christmas. Then they said it soft and tender so as to please the baby and make it smile. Now he was fair sing-songing it out to the top of his voice, still doing that little stiff clog.

> Twelve days of Christmas, sent my sweetheart
> Twelve studs a-squealin,
> Leven bulls a-bellerin,
> Ten hares a-runnin,
> Nine cows a-roarin
> Eight maids a-waitin,
> Seven swans a-swimmin,
> Six geese a-layin,
> Five goldy rings,
> Four colly birds,
> Three French hens,
> Two turkle-doves —
> AND A PATTERGE IN A PEAR-BUSH!

And he jumped and hollered out that last line, and we all squalled out like a bear was after us. Scared us plum to death. Then we all laughed and hollered and begged him to say it again. Mom snorted.

'Aw, Dad, you just a-slowing everything down, now. Hush! Here, Jean, grab this pan and throw out the water, hang up your pans and rags, chillern. We're done!'

We minded her and broke for the front room and crowded up close as we all could on the floor around the tree. The candles were lit and shining. The snow was still coming down right outside of the window, and almost it looked like it was falling on the tree. The star on the tip-top twinkled and all the tinsel sparkled in a thousand places at once, in the jumpy candlelight. That tree comes back into my memory yet, just as plain — it was so beautiful. That was about the last time we had real candles, that year, and there is something kind of holy feeling about a tree fixed like that.

Kitty called off the names on the packages, and the littlest ones who could walk delivered them around the circle. This meant May's little Alfred and Ollie's two youngest, Kathleen and Amanda. They acted mighty important, stepping about there, and they took occasion to strut and act smart, show off a little bit like children will when everybody's looking at them. I felt big, looking at them there, I remember. A year or two before I had been taking the presents around, jumping about and acting a-fool, hollering out when there was nothing to holler about, and falling down every minute or two, making out like the floor was slick just so somebody'd notice me. What a way to act! Now whenever they brought me a present, I'd grab it and say, down low, 'Look out, biggety-britches, you going to fall and make a pump-knot on your noggin, and won't be nobody's fault but yours either.' But they never let on that they heard me.

My pile of presents got bigger and bigger. I couldn't tell where in the world they had all come from, for the last time I had felt the packages under the tree, seemed like there hadn't been but a few scattering ones with my name on them. I made the paper fly every way getting them open, not like Ernestine. She untied every little string and folded up all the pretty paper, neat and lady-like. Helen and I were sitting together and we started out to do that too, but we got tired of it right away, and made as big a mess as the littler ones with the wrappings, and had just as much fun.

I got a box of handkerchiefs from Helen, but I knew about them already, what they looked like and how many there were in the box and what they cost at the store. I gave her a box just like them, with red trim where mine were blue. Mom had made me a doll cradle out of a large-size Quaker Oats box. She made it one night after I went to bed, she said, pasted the outside and the insides of it with rose-colored leaves from the wallpaper catalogue, and sewed up a real little featherbed and pillow for it. I knew what was inside them, too — down feathers out of the barrel in the cellar where she saved chicken and goose feathers to make big featherbeds out of. She had made a cover for the bed from an old lace blouse. How lovely that was to me! Like the cradle of a princess!

I began to feel pretty bad that I had given so few gifts myself. I'd put the handkerchiefs on the tree for Helen, and then I'd got some little something for Mom and for Dad. I didn't have much money in those days (this year Unie had sent me a dollar from Connecticut where she was teaching school) and nobody really expected me to give many things. But I usually got plenty of presents myself, I guess because I was the baby of the family. I kept opening one thing and another, from Edna and Kitty and Raymond and the rest, but my heart wasn't in any of them because I still had not got a doll — a pretty dollie to show off to Ernestine and Carol and Helen and Kathleen. A little tiny lump about the size of an apple seed began to bobble in my throat, and every time they brought me a little flat package that must be a pair of socks or something, that lump would get bigger and bigger.

At last all the packages were cleaned off the floor under the tree. Pauline and Jewel and Wilmer were scrambling around fishing out the gifts lodged in the pine branches, but no doll for me. The lump was big and choky, and I wanted to cry and cry, but I was ashamed to on Christmas Day with all my presents around me. Oh, I was awful sorry for myself, right then. All of a sudden there was Kitty standing in the door that led back into the front room. She was holding up a big package wrapped in brown paper. She was acting like a trainman, hollering out, 'JUST ARRIVED FROM CONNECTICUT. SPE — CHUL DELIVERY. FIRST CLASS ON THE SHORT DOG!' Everybody jumped and looked around and wondered who it might be for. I knew it was for me, and I still wanted to cry. Kitty looked at me. 'Have you been a good girl? Bless its heart, I reckon it has for once. Here now, handle it easy when you open it up — she might break!'

The bundle was so big it was all I could do to lift it. Dad got out his knife and cut the heavy strings, and helped me unwrap the first paper. There was a long, wide box, that said Boston, Massachusetts, on the lid, and the name of a store over it. I pulled away the lid, and there was soft white tissue paper in a hundred layers, all so white and clean that my hands going down among them looked grimy and frostbit. At the bottom there she was, with the sweet smile of an angel on her rosy parted lips and her eyes with their long lashes closed in sleep, there in her pure white bed. Yellow hair she had, and two tiny little teeth and the tip of her tongue you could see. She had the prettiest pink skin you ever saw. And her clothes! Her dress and her bonnet were of soft yellow silk trimmed with narrow white lace, and her petticoat was white silk trimmed in yellow. She was as big as a real girl-baby. She was from Unie, all the way from Connecticut, and Boston, and far-off places.

I picked her up all in my arms and she opened her big blue eyes and I could tell she knew me. She had the lovingest look on her face. I couldn't see another thing.

'I'm going to name her Unie Helen,' I said. I let all the others hold her and look at her, but I kept always near. I forgot all about my other presents, and I carried Unie Helen hugged up tight all the rest of the day.

After the papers and strings were all picked up and folded away in a big box to use next Christmas, we sang some more Christmas songs, only by this time most of us were getting pretty hoarse from singing and talking so much. Edna could just barely whisper, but then Edna always led all the singing and her voice every Christmas gave out before the day was half over.

While we were singing, Wilmer and Truman and Raymond and Roy Estepp slipped out on the porch and commenced shooting off firecrackers. This made Mom mad, and she fussed and railed around for a while, in and out the door. She said it was 'a pyore sacrilege and a sin and a scandal and I don't know what all, people to shoot and cut up like that on Christ's birthday.' They just laughed and told her it was a good thing they didn't get drunk and ride up and down the branch and shoot pistols, like some folks did. Granny Katty said she had heard her granddaddy say that shooting a gun was an old and honorable way of telling the people that a king was born. Mom said that it just sounded plain rukshus to her, just blasphemous. But the men shot on, anyway, until they banged away the last one of the firecrackers, then they came in and helped us finish up with 'Good Christian Men, Rejoice.' They knew that Mom liked that song.

It began to get dark out, and everybody stirred about to take another bite of this and that from the table, and plenty was still there. Ollie and Roy and their family picked up and finally got everything together, their dolls and their packages and candy, and their clothes and the like, and went off down the snowy branch and out of sight around the hill. Dad went out to get another log for the fireplace. Some sat around the table, some sat by the fire. It's a funny sort of time, that part of Christmas Day when it gets dark and everybody stops saying Merry Christmas and Christmas Gift to one another.

Then Mom and Dad said everybody was tired, been up so late the night before, and up before day that morning, why didn't we all just go to bed. Dad said he could sleep forty rows at once. I took Unie Helen and fixed up the box she came in for a bed and set it down on the floor by the big bed where I slept that night with Pauline and Jewel. I remember I longed to take her in our bed, but her dress was too pretty to wrinkle up, and they made a fuss anyway, said she took up too much room from the rest of us. Mom, over in the other bed in the room where we lay, told us to hush and go to sleep.

They got in at the head and I at the foot where I could look out the window at the stars and snow. If I turned my head on the pillow the other way I could see through the door into the dim big room where the tree stood outlined dark against the window. The low fire made little sputters of light, and I could feel on my face the room getting colder and colder. The stars and the snow looked cold too, colder than anything else I ever saw. Then the stars looked like shiny things on the biggest Christmas tree in the world, only this tree had real snow in under it, not cotton like ours had. I wondered if the stars had coats of ice over them in the wintertime, they sparkled so cold, and just thinking of it made me shiver even with all the linsey quilts over me and a featherbed beneath.

Mom and Dad were snoring, first one and then the other, high and low. I listened and heard Jewel and Pauline breathing slow and deep. I slipped off the bed and tiptoed into the big room. The pale fire lighted my way over to the dark tree. The organ squeaked awful loud when I pulled it out, though nobody woke up, so I didn't push it back.

She was as cold as the stars, poor little thing, and her skin against my arms was colder than the snow. I guess she had been on my mind all day. I was wicked and mean and the low-downdest person alive, but I was sorry for the way I had acted, and sorry for the poor little frozen poppy-doll, and God and Santy Claus could see, if they wanted to look down, that there was a little streak of good in me. I wrapped Granny's headrag well around her and warmed her in the folds of my long flannel nightgown, and we rocked backward and forward there in under the dark tree, and I cried a little into her cold brown face, and the tears shimmering there made it look like she was crying too.

'Hush and don't cry, don't cry, honey, Mommy loves you, loves you — don't cry — as much as Unie Helen. She'll name you the prettiest name, you little girl-baby. Alliefair! Do you like that? Alliefair, little Alliefair, that's what your name is. And she'll sing you a song, the prettiest song, and you'll sleep with Mommy tonight.'

I remembered all of the song, by halting some to study out

what came next, and sang it whispery to Alliefair. By the time
I had sung through up to the Ten Commandments, she was all
warm.

Children, go where I send thee;
How shall I send thee?
    I will send thee ten by ten,
        'Cause ten was the Ten Commandments,
        Nine was the nine got left behind,
        Eight was the eight that stood at the gate,
        Seven was the seven went up to Heaven,
        Six was the six that couldn't get fixed,
        Five was the guardeen angels,
        Four was the four come a-knocking at the door,
        Three was the three wise riders,
        Two was the Paul and Silas,
        One was a little bitty baby
        Wrapped in swaddlin' clothing,
        Lying in a manger.
    Born, born O! Born in Betha-lye-hem.

CHAPTER ELEVEN

*Of fall days and harvesting; of hickory nut hunting,
and stir-offs, and falling in love.*

T HE FALL of the year is a wonderful time. Give me my
choosing, and I'll take fall the whole year round, pretty
near. Of course there's work to do, getting in stuff for winter,
but fall work somehow or other never seems like it is hard. You
hitch up the old mule to the sled, go up to the fields and haul
down sledloads of corn, apples, and grapes. You can eat all you
want while you work, and get to jump on the sled and ride on
the downhill parts, coming home every load. There are great
yellow pumpkins, too, and long-neck squash — you can just
look at them piled up in the sled and see all the pies, taste the
dried squash cooked in shucky beans with a slab of ham thrown
in for flavoring, think of how good this or that pumpkin's
going to look with a funny face and a candle inside, and think

what a happy time Hallowe'en is, and Thanksgiving, too.

We would carry all the corn up the ladder into the barn loft, sort out the nubbins for the cow and mule, and store the full good ears in the other loft room against the times we'd shell and go to mill. Bam, the mule, was the proudest thing and got so he wouldn't eat nubbins, and then he had to have six or seven of these good ears a day, too. Dad said he reckoned Bam figured, here he was doing all that work plowing and helping raise that corn, and then hauling it down from the fields, so that he might as well get the best of it — no more than his due. One winter I remember Dad fed old Bam so well that we had to borrow corn from Aunt Mary Ann, enough for a turn or two, to do us for corn bread until the crop came in that next summer.

On Saturdays we'd get up before the birds and go a hickory-nut hunting, take flour sacks and coffee sacks and stay all the long day rambling about in the hills. Mom would go with us, and was the best climber among us, too. We'd race and chase up ahead of her, and get so winded that we'd have to fall down and rest. By the time we'd start on, she'd be up with us. She'd never stop until she got to the top of the ridge, then she'd stand still and puff a little, fanning herself with a cowcumber leaf and looking all around her.

'Lord, children, look what a pretty sight it is. I guess it's Indian Summer. My dad allus said you couldn't find anything so fair as an Indian Summer day. The air right hazy soft and the sunshine yaller as firelight, and the hills all manner of fine colors.'

Whenever Mom talked like that and looked away off it made me feel like she was talking to someone far away there where she was looking, someone I knew and yet did not know. I'd get around and pull at her apron so she would notice me. I'd get the same feeling whenever I went to church with her, and they started singing those old long slow lonesome songs. She'd sing and the tears would start in her eyes and she'd forget all about me there beside her. It was like she had gone off and left me, it was the lonesomest feeling. Once I asked her why all the church songs sounded so sad, and why it was she always cried in church. She said:

'Folks in church cries for joy, not because they are sad. The singing, well, 'pears to me like our songs are the only real good music I ever did hear. Lot of churches you go to now, sing them little flibberty-te-jibbity songs, sound more like dance pieces than meeting songs. Our meeting-house songs are different. I purely love them in my heart, love to dwell on the words of them, relish the tune of them. To me they are more like worship and God than any other music.'

I guess the way she felt in church and the way she felt in the midst of the fall hills must have been somehow akin to each other, but I couldn't appreciate that at the time. I was only worried because she wouldn't look at me. Anyway, she finally would notice, in a minute or two and ask me how many hickory nuts we had found.

'Is that all you got? Swear to goodness I thought you'd know where the good trees stand. Take over in the holler yonder, that old twisted tree that was struck by lightning, see if it's got any this year. I'm satisfied that's the one allus bears the best of any around here.'

Walnuts we'd gather too, long walnuts and black walnuts. They tasted the best of any kind of nuts when we made fudge on winter evenings after supper. The very best taste of all, though, was to crack out a handful of black walnuts and eat them with a piece of cold corn bread, first a bit of nut and then a bite of bread. That's the main best eating in the world!

There was no end of good things about the fall. Often we'd get out of school in fodder-pulling time, for the teacher couldn't say much when your own mom and dad said you had to stay home and pull fodder. Then there was the excitement of storing up the apples in under the floor so that the whole house smelled like a party all winter long. Or helping to make jelly out of the grapes and apple butter out of the apples that wouldn't keep, and getting to scrape all the pans. Or looking for the prettiest bunch of fall leaves to put on the teacher's desk at school. Or getting a new pair of shoes because it'd soon be cold weather.

More partying, too, in the fall. I guess that was the time when the reasons for parties were most plentiful. Stir-offs, pie suppers, corn gatherings, and other kinds of workings with one thing and another about the harvest, always winding up with everybody playing games and singing and running a few sets.

It was in the fall, just before my fourteenth birthday, that I first fell in love.

I was a big, healthy, gangly girl, not slim and not pretty. I was good in my books and everybody thought well of me, but the boys never winked at me or pulled my straight red hair. They never said much of anything at all to me, come to think of it. Seemed like they were afraid of me, and I was scared finally to death of them. I was so bashful that whenever a boy looked at me sideways, my tongue would cleave to the roof of my mouth and my face would turn every which color. The worst of it was that everybody saw how bad I felt about it and every living soul I knew began to tease and torment the life out of me over the boys. Seems like that would just fly all over me, and I'd light into them, whoever'd tease me, and I'd just want to kill them, scratch out their eyeballs and pull out their hair by the roots.

Mom would say, 'Now what you reckon makes her act thataway? Why she's been claiming the boys all of her life, bragging about how this one and that one was her sweetheart. What's got into her now?'

Then she'd be bound to tell about the time when I was just five years old, I came running into the kitchen house where she was stirring up some bread for supper.

'Well Mommie, I know who it is I'm a-going to marry when I get big.'

'You do now! Lordy mercy, who is it?'

'Nobody but Little-Bill Browning.'

'That's a mighty fine thing to know, little girl. How'd you find out about it?'

'He ast me!'

Now, here I was going on fourteen and in my heart I wanted more than anything to be noticing the boys, but they just didn't like me. They all acted like it plagued them to talk with me, like I wasn't good enough for them, and they were ashamed to be seen with me. I thought I knew why it was. It was on account of the way I looked. I wasn't little and slim like the other girls were, and I never had any new clothes. Everything I wore had belonged to several other people before it got down to me.

I began to act as though I couldn't stand the boys, would fight anyone who named one to me, and said nobody'd ever catch me walking and talking with any of them. That was another thing — I couldn't talk. In my mind I could have charming talks with rich handsome men, have them fighting duels with each other over me, right and left, but whenever I undertook to say any of those smart things to the boys I knew, the pretty words came out all wrong. The boys would look at me and say yes or no, if they bothered to say that much, and then they'd go away.

One day in October I was sitting at my desk in school, studying my lessons, when someone eased into the seat beside me. I looked up, thinking to see Helen or one of the other girls, but there was Cleve Hamilton with a grin all over his face and a twinkle in his blue eyes, acting like he wasn't a bit afraid of me. Cleve was the only boy in school who didn't have to do a blessed thing to get the girls to notice him. They were all so crazy about him that he just had to look at them once, and they'd take the big-head for a week.

He was the best basketball player in the whole school. He was tall and slim but with plenty of muscles; he had the curliest light-colored hair, and every move he made put you in mind of a streak of lightning. I thought he was the prettiest thing in the world, but I hated him because he was stuck-up, and I never even thought of wanting him to talk to me because I knew he never would.

My first thought was to jump up and run away. He put his arm around the back of the seat.

'Howdy Cleve,' I said. My insides were on fire. I tried to hide my red face with the geography book. Cleve peeped over the edge. He had to whisper because it was in time of books.

'Tell me what in tarnation you studying about so hard?'

'Geography.'

'Never saw anyone study so hard as you do. Here shut up that fool book and talk to me.'

I determined that I wouldn't let him scare me to death, so I looked him right in the face and eyes and asked him what it was he had to say.

Cleve let out a big laugh, and the teacher frowned and said, 'Sh-h-h!'

'Well, don't look so all-fired mad, I ain't going to ask you to shoot yer granny. I just want to be friendly like.'

He came closer so nobody could hear but me, and the look on his face put me in mind of a little boy.

'Honey, I like you and you won't ever look my way at all. Maybe that's the reason I like you, but what's the matter, don't you like menfolks or are you just bashful?'

'I'm ugly!' I whispered. I don't remember ever saying that to anyone before and I felt right good about it. Cleve looked like I was crazy.

'Why, honey, you're not ugly. What makes you say a thing like that, you — you — redhead!'

'It's awful to be a redhead. Little young uns follow you around, say,

"Redhead, gingerbread,
Five cents a cabbage head!"'

Well, in no time we were both laughing and joking and everything I said was coming out just right. Came time for the geography and for the first time I didn't know a one of the answers. A funny thing about that was, Mr. Hall didn't seem to mind. Once I looked up quick and caught him smiling down at Cleve and me, for all the world like he knew a good secret.

That evening I went home from school and threw down my books, and took to the hills to hunt the cows without anyone telling me to go. I raced through the woods like a deer, swinging on grapevines and tree limbs, and laughing and making speeches on top of high rocks, and cutting such a shine that I was ashamed of myself, but that nor nothing else could stop me. The old cow was waiting for me at the gap, and I let down the bars with a great clatter and hollered, 'HEIGH!' at her so loud that she must have thought I was plum crazy, for she swung her old head around and looked at me a minute and then heisted her tail and made the dirt and rocks just fly getting down that hill road, her bell clangety-bang-banging like the devil was after her.

I marched down the road behind her with my stick over my shoulder, singing to the top of my lungs. I never usually hollered out on a song like some folks around did, but now I purely felt like it. A funny thing was that I was singing, the best I remember, 'Come All Ye Fair.' The words of that song surely didn't match my feeling, but maybe the tune did, or maybe it was just because it was a song you could really holler out on, and to me at that time it seemed like the finest song in the world.

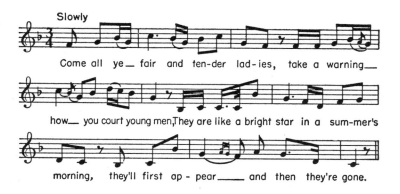

Come all ye fair and tender ladies,
Take a warning how you court young men;
They are like a bright star in a summer's morning,
They'll first appear and then they're gone.

They'll tell to you some lovely story,
They'll 'clare to you their love is true,
Straightaway they'll go and court some other
And that is the love they have for you.

I wisht I was some little sparrow
And I had wings and I could fly,
I'd fly away to my false truelover,
And while they'd talk I'd sit and cry.

But I am not no little sparrow,
I have no wings and I can't fly;
So I'll sit right here in my grief and sorrow,
And pass my troubles by and by.

If I had a known before I courted
That love had a-been such a killing thing,
I'd a-locked my heart in a chest of golden
And a-bound it down with a silver pin.

Young man, ne'er cast your eye on beauty,
For beauty is a thing that will decay;
I've seen many a fair and a bright sunny morning
Turn into a dark and deludinous day.

Aunt Mary Ann heard the racket and came out on her porch, and I could tell by the way she stood there with her hands on her hips and looked up the hill at me going by, I could tell that she was wondering what on earth had come over me. I thought to myself, right now Aunt Mary Ann is saying to Oly, 'Why that's Balis's young un going long up there. Swear I reckon he's a-raising him up a right wild girl.'

That night after we got supper over and the dishes washed we all were sitting around in the front room, doing one thing and another. I was trying to get my lessons, but I couldn't to save my neck do a thing but write Cleve Hamilton's pretty name over every page I turned. Dad came stomping in off the back porch with a great log for the fire. He threw it on the fire in just the right place and a thousand sparkles cracked out and sailed up the chimney.

'Shore is a fall time out tonight. Makes me wish I had a little patch of cane — might near the best stirrin-off weather I ever seed.'

I got a quivering breath and my heart near failed me at the thoughts of a stir-off. I'd make Cleve go and we would stand in the dark and talk, like the other girls and their boys did. I never said a word, though. I felt like if I cleared my throat everybody would know what was in my mind, and they'd start to shame me and make fun.

'I know who's raising cane this year,' Mom looked up from the Bible she was reading, half-ways smiling, teasing us.

'Hunh. Who wouldn't know that!' Wilmer said. 'It's Lee-up-on-the-Branch. I saw that cane patch when the cows broke out of the pasture one day last month and I had to hunt them up the left-hand fork. Went all the way up to Lee's fore I heard their bells, and I passed a right pretty patch of green cane.'

'Don't get too brash now,' Dad warned. 'Maybe he's a-keeping it a secret. Maybe he don't aim to have a stir-off for everybody.'

'Well, the secret's out now, I already told a lot of boys about it, and we won't let him stir-off by himself now!' Wilmer laughed.

Sure enough, one day not long after that, Dosh Brashear, Lee's woman, passed by on her way from the store to her house a mile up the branch, and she stopped to talk awhile with Mom like she always did. She said they had gathered in the cane, and tomorrow they would gin it. If all went according to plan, they'd stir-off just after dark the next evening. As she went out of sight at the big cliff in the curve of the branch, she thought to holler back, 'We had a right smart patch this year, so you'ns can bring your bucket!'

Next day at school when Cleve came to my seat, I let him know in a roundabout way that I was going to a stir-off that night. He said that was funny, he was going to the same one.

'I reckon I'll see you there, then,' he said. 'If I do, will you talk with me?'

'I been brought up to be civil to everybody, mister.'

'Aw, you know what I mean. You just better be there, that's all!'

As I recall those days, it was the craziest feeling I had about Cleve. I liked him and I didn't. I liked him whenever he sat in my seat at school and all the other girls saw us and wished they had him. But I didn't like him when he'd come and butt in on the games we girls were playing at recess, or when he'd catch me drawing paper dolls and laugh at me. I liked for the girls to see him put his arm around the back of my seat and hug me a little before I could stop him. It tickled me for them all to see it, but it really would make me mad for him to do that, and when I'd get mad and tell him he better stop I meant it. I couldn't stand for him even to touch my hand. It was a strange thing, in my heart I wanted him to touch me, I would dream day and night about him holding my hand, about how it would be to comb his curly head with my fingers. I would dream and tremble with pleasure, but as soon as he would get near to me and take hold of my hand I would get mad and begin to fight him, say mean things, and tell him to let me alone. Then he'd laugh and call me his little wildcat, but after a while, three or four weeks after he first began to pay attention to me, I began to catch him looking at me when he thought I wasn't noticing, in a way that caused me to be afraid.

The day of the stir-off was a Friday, and school let out early for some reason. On the way home Sallie suggested that some of us go up early and watch Lee-up-on-the-Branch gin his cane. Mom said I could go, but we must just watch and not get in the way of the work. Pauline and Jewel and Wilmer would come on up after dark. Mom came out on the porch and hollered after us.

'You'ns keep your feet dry now, for it's late in the year and you'll sure catch a cold if you don't. Walk on the rocks whenever the road goes through the water. As I recollect, that left-hand fork road runs along ever so fur right smack dab in the creek bed. Don't sass anybody, and help if they want you to.'

I had on my prettiest blue dress, and my hair tied back with a big blue ribbon because Cleve was coming. But I clear forgot about Cleve as soon as we started racing each other up the branch. For a while we tried to see which one could outrun the others, then we played banner. Sallie's baby brother, Cotton, was the banner and he led us through thickets of blackberry briers and all manner of places like that, and we had to follow him or we'd be out. He walked the footlogs on their tip edges and he jumped the branch in the widest parts. We did everything that he did until just before we got to Lee's he bannered all of us girls by doing skin-the-cat on a tree limb. We all had dresses on and couldn't do it.

'There's where at they're ginning! Down there in the big bottom yonder!'

'Yeh boy, look at that old mule going round and round. I'll beat you all down!'

We sailed down that mountainside like we had wings. There was Lee watching the cane juice squeeze out into the pans, and emptying out the full ones into the big long stirring-off pan over the pit. They were almost done ginning. There was already a fire blazing in the pit, and two of Lee's boys were feeding the last scattered bunches of cane stalks into the gin.

'Why howdy, chillern. Little early now. Help yourselves to some good juicy cane stalks to suck on, then you can help dig the skimming hole. You've come in fine time for that.'

Lee-up-on-the-Branch pointed to a place not far from the pit where he wanted to have his skimming hole dug. We all stood around sucking our cane stalks and taking time-about, digging with the pick and shovel. Everybody was making big plans about who he would push into the skimming hole before the night was out.

'Dig her wide and dig her deep there, feller. You don't want your legs cramped none whenever you get pushed into her tonight!'

'Hunh. Nobody won't have to shove *you* in, knucklehead. You got such a little understanding, you'll just flounder in 'thout being shoved!'

'Me, I'd like to see Jean here fall in. Like to see that purty blue dress all dripping with them old 'lasses skimming. Wonder would Clevie love her so well then!'

'You don't hush up, Mr. Fred Hall, you going to get into that hole fore she gets finished. Smarty.'

'Wait'll atter moonrise, we'll see who's first.'

The sky darkened and the hoot owls began to holler along the black ridges. If you looked away from the fire, up through the woods to the deep, deep gray sky and the cold pale stars, and heard the owls and other night birds singing their doleful songs, why then it seemed like a mighty scary, lonesome place to be in. Then you looked back quick at the bright blazing fire and the sweet molasses bubbling soft green-yellow bubbles in the big pan, and boys and girls laughing and chasing one another, and lantern lights along the high hill road bringing more and more folks to the party. That was a beautiful sight, and the warm brightness of it folded in around you and kept you from the dark.

It was time to skim the molasses. Lee took the skimmer, a great wooden spoon with a handle four or five feet long, and passed it along the top of the bubbling mass. He dipped off as much as he could of the green jellyish skim which lay on the top, and the boys emptied it, with devilish grins on their faces, into the skimming hole. I began to chew up one end of a cane stalk and spread the chewed end out into a nice brush, to be ready to dip into the pan. That is one of the best tastes on earth. You dip your cane stalk down into the boiling pan, catch the yellow foam on the end of the stalk, wave it in the air until it's cooled down some, and suck it off. Again and again you dip it in, for once you start there's no stopping. It's far better than the finished molasses; the taste of it puts you in mind of fall winds and wood smoke and dancing in the fields, and games played in the secret dark.

Lee saw me fixing my stalk and laughed a big laugh. 'Here now, here's a little girl going to eat her skimmings green! You put away that stick for at least another hour or two, have to skim another time or two yet fore the skimmings get yellow. Green foam'll make you sick sure.'

The young folks heard that and they started to work fixing a place to run a set. They made everybody help.

'Here, let's yank up these old stalks and stomp us down a level place. Here, you little ones, get to trompling, you got nothing else to do, stomp it until it's just like a floor.'

'They hain't no music come yet, Wint. Can't run a set 'thout music. Not a solitary fiddle amongst us.'

'Shucks, they'll be a fiddle or a banjer or something turn up soon. Anyway, reckon we can play "Cedar Swamp" right now. Get you a gal and don't be bashful, and mind the skimmin' hole!'

I had been wishing in the back of my mind all evening long that Cleve wouldn't come. It would be no fun at a stir-off, I decided, if I had to stand around and talk to an old boy all evening and not get to run and wrestle with the young uns as I was used to. Besides, now we had been rolling and tumbling about, so that my pretty blue dress was wrinkled and the hem was torn with the briers. My ribbon was gone and my long hair was blown about my face and I had to keep brushing it back with my hands. I was one of the children — and mighty glad of it — not old enough to court.

But when they commenced lining up for 'Cedar Swamp,' I wanted to play. I stood with the other littler ones and wished someone would ask me to play, but no one did. Someone whispered, 'Where's Cleve at?' and I wanted to die. Now everybody would think he had made it up with me to come, and then disappointed me.

Above the singing voices and dancing feet I heard the clear high sound. Faraway it was, and so faint that the sound of it sometimes got lost, but there was no mistaking what it was.

At last they heard it too.

'Hush boys, hush a while. Swear if I don't hear that old fiddle a-whinin' down the holler som'ers!'

'Whose bow is it? Chad McDaniel's?'

'Naw, nary a bit like Chad. Hush, there 'tis. More like Cleve's.'

'Cleve Hamilton. That's who it is. That young un can really play. What's his tune? Listen. Hush.'

'Favors "Napoleon Crossing the Rockies." Is it? Listen.'

'Can't you fellers hear it thunder?' Dad said. Dad was known to be hard of hearing, but I guess he just had an ear for music. He said, 'I can hear plain as day, that chap is playing "Goin' To See My Truelove."'

He began to hum and fool with the song, and some joined in:

> The days are long and lonesome,
> The nights are a-gettin' cold;
> I'm goin' to see my truelove
> 'Fore I get too old.
>
>> O get around, Jenny, get around,
>> O get around I say,
>> O get around, Jenny, get around,
>> Long summer day.
>
> I went up on the mountain
> Give my horn a blow,
> I thought I heard that pretty girl
> Say: 'Yonder comes my beau!'
>
> Ast that gal to marry me,
> Tell you what she said.

Freely

1. The days are long and lone-some, the nights are a-get-tin' cold; I'm
goin' to see my true love 'fore I get too old.

CHORUS, with a steady beat

O get a-round, Jen-ny, get a-round, O get a-round I say,

O get a-round,— Jen-ny, get a-round, long—sum-mer day.

Picked her up a knotty pine stick
And like to broke my head.

I went up on the mountain
Give my horn a blow,
If I can't get the gal I want
Let that ole gal go.

I went up on the mountain
Get me a load of pine,
Loaded my wagon so heavy
Broke it down behind.

Met a raccoon in the road
Mad as he could be,
Quiled his tail and whupped my dog
And bristled up at me.

Well, when I heard Cleve's fiddle playing that tune, I began
to brighten up. I must have looked better because Jim Hall

came over right then and asked me to dance with him. It made me proud to be dancing when Cleve came into the firelight. I was glad I wasn't standing with the little children, looking on.

Then Cleve played for the sets, and it seemed like that fiddle music turned the devil loose among the boys. One of them would be standing beside of his girl, patting his foot and clapping and waiting his time to dance out, then the dancing couples would go by him, and next minute, splop! there he'd be up to his shins in the skimming hole, mad and sputtering. I guess they finally had shoved all the boys and one or two of the tomboy girls into that hole before Lee finally hollered out to us.

'Here, young uns, run dip in your stalks. Prettiest yellow foam you ever did see. Dip in, dip in there, and eat all you can. Ollie, Abbie, hand me your buckets here. This foam'll settle to more'n half molasses, you'll see.'

Aunt Mary Ann said, 'Just fill my bucket halfways up, Lee. I know this ain't the last skimmin', I'll finish filling it whenever you skim her for the main last time. That's the best foam.'

'Why, yes, I guess you will! The last skimmin'll be most all of it pure molasses. Well, I don't reckon I mind giving a good neighbor a quart of molasses. There'll be some for sale in the wintertime and I'll get a good price out of you for it, lady!'

I had forgot about my feller again, and was down at the foot of the big pan with Cotton and Kathleen and little Amanda, eating 'lasses foam to beat the band. Cleve came up behind me and pulled me by the ends of my long hair up and away from the others. He looked mad.

'Well, do you want to see me or not? Fine way to treat someone. Here you run off and I had to walk up this long dark holler all by myself — '

'You scared of the dark?'

'No, I'm not scared of the dark, but just the same I don't know the road much well, almost fell head fo'most off'n that high bank where the slip is, stepped in the creek up to my knees, kept hearing all kind of strange noises in the woods, seeing eyes looking at me — '

'Wonder the hants didn't get you. Wisht they had!'

'Spiteful! Then I get up here, and there you are dancing with everybody else, and me having to play the fiddle all the time, and then you won't even offer to feed me off'n your cane stalk, you set down here eating like a little pig, and now you stand there laughing at me. I ought to whup you, that's what I ought to do.'

We both were laughing then and I began to like him again. At last he whispered in my ear. 'Come walk with me.'

'Whereabouts?'

'Over yonder, anywhere, where they can't spy us. Never did like to stand and talk to my girl in front of everybody.'

'What's wrong with talking in front of people? They won't care.'

'Aw, come on. Look around. Most of the others are off walking and talking out there in the field. What're you afraid of, little baby?'

'I said I'd talk with you but I didn't promise to walk.'

'You're my girl, ain't you? If you're not now, I want you to be my girl. Then walk with me a little.'

'Well, just to the edge of the dark there. Now, what do you have to say that's so blessed important?'

'I don't know now. You look right pretty tonight, with your hair blowing back wild like that on the night wind —'

'I lost my hair ribbon, running with the others —'

'And your pretty blue dress that I love so well, that fits you so neat —'

'I tore it in the berry briers, playing banner with the children —'

'You look like a little girl, and yet like a woman grown, and the sight of you takes out of mind all the things I had to say to you —'

'Here we are on the edge of the dark. Take me back —'

'No, no, look on out there in the fields. It's not dark out there, it just seemed so when you were by the fire. The full moon is halfway the sky, how can it be dark?'

He had hold of my hand and we stood still. I trembled for a while but he said not a word. Then he said listen to the wind in the ridges, and the hoot owls calling out bad news, and he said look at the stars and how pretty the moon is, and after a while I stopped trembling. Back at the fire someone hollered out.

'All right, we going to play five-ten. I'll count first and everybody hide, but not more'n a hundred feet away!'

The voice began to chant,

> Five, ten, fifteen, twenty,
> Twenty-five, thirty, thirty-five, forty —

'Come on, let's hide together. I know a place — ' We began to run.

> Forty-five, fifty, fifty-five, sixty,
> Sixty-five, seventy, seventy-five, eighty —

'Cleve! Stop it, stop, we're way over a hundred feet — '
'Right here. Old fodder stack, nobody'll look for us here!'

> Eighty-five, ninety, ninety-five, hundred.

> Bushel of wheat, bushel of rye,
> All ain't hid, holler 'I.'

> Bushel wheat, bushel cotton,
> All ain't hid, better be a-trottin'!

> Bushel wheat, bushel clover,
> All ain't hid, can't hide over!

We ran stumbling and panting hard to the fodder stack and fell down behind it. We were both laughing so hard we were afraid the counter would hear us, and I couldn't stop laughing at all, so that Cleve clapped his hand over my mouth to keep me quiet.

I had never before been so close to any boy. I sat leaning my back against him, very quiet, and it seemed like I had a hundred hearts all inside of me trying to get out. I didn't have the power to move, to do any more than breathe, but I wasn't resting easy. I kept trying to act to myself like it was Kathleen or Cotton or some of the others there behind me. If it was one of them I wouldn't be shaking and shivering this way, it would just be fun, hiding there in the dark. But I couldn't forget it was Cleve. The hand holding my mouth was the shape and the smell of Cleve's hand, the breath that moved the body behind was his breath.

Out there in the moonlighted field the counter roamed about in the shadowy places. He'd see someone and then they'd break in a race for the counting tree. Sometimes the words that rolled over the field would be, 'One-two-three for Pauline!' and again they would be, 'In free! In free! One-two-three for me!' Their voices and laughing and the sound of their running came clear to us and seemed very near, but the counter never came over as far as our fodder stack.

I heard the sounds of the game as though they were dream sounds. Everything I could see and hear around me seemed so queer, it was like the whole world was changing away from me, everything was different, nothing was real. This morning I had dreamed of being near to Cleve, now here it was and I didn't like it. It was the feeling inside of me that came along with being alone with him that I didn't like. I didn't know what to do with it. I had never had this kind of feeling before. There was almost something nice about it, but I was afraid and miserable and wanted to cry. I kept having to swallow for no reason and the sound of my swallowing was louder than the beating of my heart. I knew Cleve could hear and I was shamed to death. He'd think I was a fool and a baby.

His hand moved away from my mouth, over my face and forehead and smoothed on my hair. He put his other arm around my waist. I sat there stiff as a board, wanting to holler out and yet wanting to let him hold me; wanting to run away and wanting to stay. I remember that most of my mind was to run, but some stubborn thing or other made me want to stay even against my liking. It was something inside of me that had to know what this strange feeling was, had to find out things everlastingly. So when he turned my face to him, I sat still and waited. He leaned over quick and kissed me on the mouth. I just looked at him right straight for a while, kind of foolish. I thought I was going to cry sure, I was so disappointed. Everybody'd talked and carried on about kissing and hugging, why there wasn't a thing in the world to it anyway.

'You like that there kiss, honey?' Cleve looked anxious.

'Well, I don't know hardly. You better kiss me again.'

He did it different this time, slower and softer. He wouldn't stop. I jumped up and lit out across the fields before he could come to himself. I wiped my mouth hard with my hand. I couldn't wait to get to some water and wash my mouth out good. Cleve was running after me now, I could hear him brushing against the crackly cane stalks, stumbling over the dried clods, cussing mad. I was mad too. Why had folks led me to believe that love was so wonderful, that a kiss was such a pleasure? I was glad, too, as I ran. Let the boys chase me, or not, I wouldn't care either way. I could be scornful of them all now that I was free of their spell. I laughed out loud at the moon, and all at once I was almost up to the fire and the young uns were motioning me to be careful or the counter would see me.

'Lay low, lay low!' they chanted out. I glanced behind me and saw that Cleve had stopped in the field and was rolling him a cigarette like he never had a thought of running after me. I dropped to the earth and watched the counter looking about for me. It was Sallie, and at last she strayed away from the counting tree and I saw I could make it.

'Come in, come in!' I heard them call. I rose and made for the tree and beat Sallie to it and got in free. She looked around a while longer, then she gave up finding the rest of the hiders. She cupped her hands and hollered.

'Bee, bee, bumble bee, all's outs in free!'

'Why, who else is out? Nobody but Cleve. Now where could he be?'

'Aw, he's not even playing,' I said.

Some of the older folks had begun to stir around to go home; they gathered their buckets and their little children and lit their lanterns. They said, 'Go home with us why don't you?' and 'Can't tonight, I reckon. You'ns come,' to each other, and pretty soon their lights were fading this way and that way through the hills. The fire in the pit was low, almost ashes. Some of the boys were staying around to put it out, and to wash up the stir-off vessels. Over to one side the good-smelling molasses was cooling in a row of big shiny milk buckets. It would taste mighty fine along in the wintertime when all the green plenty of the garden stuff was gone. Dad would take his whole meal on it, just about. He would take a big spoonful of molasses and let it run thick and slow over fresh-churned butter in a dish, then he'd take his fork and mix and stir, make Gray Horse to eat on his corn bread. Hot corn bread, or biscuits, either one it would go with fine.

The young folks were leaving now. They lingered about the fire long enough for their families to get a head start and then the sweethearts began to pair off down the holler and through the woods. I got with Kathleen and Cotton and Amanda and wouldn't let them game along too much, for I didn't want to see Cleve. I might have to let him take me home. We hurried along in the dark and we'd catch up with one light after another and pass the sweethearts by. Pauline and Bingham, Helen and Chad, Ernestine and Buford, Sallie and Jerry.

I got to wondering whereabouts Cleve was. My mouth still burnt me, and I knew that if I got in the light too much everybody could see where Cleve had kissed me. I was as sure as I ever was of anything that my mouth didn't look the same. Every time we passed one of the lanterns I'd keep away to the side of the light and turn my head to the dark. What would I do tomorrow when I had to face the light of day, what would I do and say? How on earth could I hide it? That worried me more the farther down the branch we got and I walked quiet. The others were getting sleepy-eyed and they began to sniffle and fuss and whine for their mommies. What babies! Couldn't even stay awake on their own feet and it not midnight. At last I couldn't stand their trifling little ways any longer. I decided to walk faster and catch up with Mom, then I decided to walk slower and watch for Cleve. Not that I wanted to walk with him, but I was peevish because he didn't seem to be trying to find me.

The fiddle sung out then, far back up the dark holler, not a dancy tune now. A slow-like tune, a lonesome love tune. Sometimes it sailed clear up to the night sky and sometimes it sunk down and got lost in the branch waters. All at once I had a frightening thought that the music was a living thing, lost and crying, the fiddle bow making little slides and quavers and trembles all around the tune, like teardrops. Every note of it seemed to light in my breast; I was that song.

The sound came nearer and nearer, and my steps fell slower, keeping time, and as Cleve came up to my side, the words came and sang themselves inside of me.

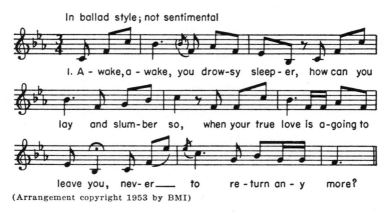

(Arrangement copyright 1953 by BMI)

> Awake, awake, you drowsy sleeper,
>   How can you lay and slumber so
> When your truelove is a-going to leave you
>   Never to return any more?

How can you slumber on your pillow
  When your truelove must stand and wait,
And must I go and wear the willow
  In sorrow mourning for your sake?

O Molly dear, go ask your Mother
  If you my bride, my bride can be,
And then return and quickly tell me
  And I no more shall trouble thee.

O no, I cannot ask my Mother,
  Such stories of love she will not hear;
Go on your way and court some other,
  I must not trouble Mother dear.

O Molly dear, go ask your Father
  If you my bride, my bride can be,
And then return and quickly tell me
  And I no more shall trouble thee.

O no, I cannot ask my Father,
  He's a-lying on his bed of rest,
And in his hands is a silver dagger
  To pierce the one that I love the best.

I wish I was in some lonely valley
  Where no one could ever hear,
My food would be the grief and sorrow
  My drink would be the briny tear.

Down in yon valley there grows a green arrow,
  I wish that arrow was shot through my breast,
It would end my grief, it would end my sorrow,
  And set my troubled mind at rest.

*Marriage, birth, and death within the family: An account
of May's wedding, a very fine and proper affair, this
account followed with the telling of how Patty kept
an angel for a little while, and then took him back to
Heaven.*

M Y SISTER Ollie was the first one to marry, of the ten
girls, but May followed soon after, and she was the
first one to have a big wedding. When she told me about the
wedding she went farther back and remembered some things
about her courting days.

The yellowing snapshots of her wedding show her as a tall,
well-built girl, shy and pretty, her long hair — honey-red it
was — waving softly about her face and caught up in buns at

the nape of her neck in the then latest fashion. Her face is soft and smiley, but something in the square of her jaw and the way her eyes look out at you from the picture show that she is a girl used to having her way.

'It was certainly a hard matter for me to get married,' she said, 'for I never liked the boys when I was growing up. One could look at me, or just speak to say howdy, and I thought he might be liking me, I'd get so embarrassed I couldn't do a thing. Then I'd get so mad at them for following me around that I'd not pay the least attention to them, only seemed like that would make them that much worse. Ollie, now, seems like she was more lively than I ever was in that way, she went out of her way to be nice to the boys. Why, she'd not think a thing of walking and talking with them, or inviting them to the house on a Sunday. When several of them would come around that way, I'd hide in the back room or among the apple trees in the orchard behind the house, and not come in.

'And then, if I *did* get up enough nerve to walk with a boy, if a soul made fun of him the least bit, or teased me at all, I just couldn't ever like that boy again. I don't know whatever made me turned like that. I couldn't stand for anyone to think that I liked the boys.

'Like one Sunday at Bertha Campbell's house, the young people all gathered in to pass the time with one another with talking and laughing and a little music, a little teasing around like young folks follows doing. It got going-home time, and one of the boys there would be to walk home with me. Wasn't a thing I could do to turn him back, so we started home. My face was just as red, I could feel it afire, and I was mad too, but he talked so nice and so polite that I had about got over my mad spell by the time we got in sight of home. When we got to the little footlog over the branch, though, I made him stop because there sat Dad reading on the front porch. Well, my feller wouldn't go right away, stood around there and talked awhile, trying to get my promise to go somewheres with him the next Sunday. Dad, he kept glancing up from his paper without letting on that he was watching, and I got more nervous all the time. Finally, I said I might go with him and he left, and I came on into the yard. Dad kept on reading like he hadn't seen me yet. As I walked up the steps he kind of rattled his paper and said, 'Whyn't you bring your long-nosed feller to the house?' Ever after that, that boy's nose seemed to be the biggest part about him and I never would look at him again, for all that he was so run-after by all the other girls around.

'I went off to the Settlement School at Pine Mountain, finished up school and worked there awhile. Seems like I was always running away from some boy or other, would always tell Mom and Dad I was not interested in any man, nor getting married. Then word went around the school that a young man from Belgium across the waters was coming to stay and work at the school. He had a funny name, Leon Deschamps. The day he came I had to get his room ready, then when he got there I showed him to the room and said as few words as I could to him, I was so bashful. He began right away to pay attention to me, and I just could not stand him. But he wouldn't give up so easy. He even came home to see me one summer when I was home for a vacation.

'About the time he came to see me that time, it was a little after the World's War, and in the locality around home some Italians and some other foreigners had been settling. Most of them were poor folks, they spoke a strange tongue and kept to themselves. Some were dirty about their housekeeping and a few were caught stealing. Anyway, everybody was more'n a little bit afraid of them. So when Leon came to our house, the family couldn't think of a thing but him being a foreigner, and they acted uneasy. But I'd laugh around and tell them all he didn't mean a thing to me, that I didn't invite him to come to see me. After he was gone, one evening Dad walked into the kitchen, threw down his load of wood in the box, blew his nose, and said, "I'd as lief see one of my young uns dead as married to a furriner." "Who's marrying one?" I snapped out at him.

'Well, after I did decide to marry Leon I worried a lot about Dad saying that and I was afraid to tell him. At last I wrote to Mom, "My mind is made up; I aim to marry this man. He is a good man, and there is no one can change me about him." Mom wrote back the same advice and the only advice she has given to all of us, "If you love him, marry him. If you think it would be a pleasure to wash his dirty socks, then you love him." It must have been a shock to Dad, though, for Mom says that he never spoke a word when he read the letter, nor for a whole day and night after.

'We got married here in Viper, in our front yard, in the spring. It was a white wedding, and many folks in the country round had never seen such a one. The women at Pine Mountain, Mrs. Zande and the others, they thought the world of both of us, and we of them. They got together and made all my wedding clothes, sewed every stitch of them by hand. My dress was white, made in tiers down to my ankles, and they made the prettiest little veil "for your pretty hair" as they said. A traveling dress they made, and such beautiful underclothes! I have never before nor since owned such pretty things. Embroidered and tucked and trimmed with dainty handmade lace.

'The Pine Mountain people all rode over for the wedding day. On the way, Mrs. Zande's horse threw her and she broke her ankle, but she wouldn't be outdone by that, climbed back up and rode that horse on in over the mountains. We bandaged that ankle right tight and she said she felt fine, and insisted on letting it go until after the wedding celebration was over. Leon had a friend come all the way from Lexington to be the best man, and I think to the children he was as much of a curiosity as Leon, Lexington seemed so far away. Ollie had already married then, and she and her man Roy were there, and all of the Viper neighbors, and the kin from Knott County.'

Here Mallie put in her word, 'Gee-oh! I wouldn't have that time to go through again for nothing in this world. That was the awfullest feeling, all those strange fine people there, so many to cook for and the old stove a-running out of wood every minute, and us all so afraid the fare wouldn't be fancy enough for the company. I was burning up with shame because Dad forgot to get my new shoes he had promised and I had to wear my old clumsy black ones that looked all out of place with the thin organdy dress I had made myself.

'Seems like I could just feel those people from nice rich places, looking around and noticing how shabby everything was, how poor the Ritchies were, and how make-shifty. We were all praying that Leon wouldn't look under his bed and see how we had built a rest for his bedsprings out of empty wooden boxes! I couldn't see how Leon, that fine man from off, could ever bring himself to have his wedding in such a lowly place. What must they all think of us and the house and our country ways and all the noisy children? I felt so shamed that the Lexington man had to ruin his shoes on the dusty, rocky road up the branch, him that was used to smooth side-walks. I felt like going right down into the ground whenever anybody looked at me all day long, and I vowed a vow that none of the others would ever get married at home if I could help it, if they married fine people, that is.'

'Well, Mallie, you were the only one a-suffering much over things like that,' May laughed. 'I didn't get that feeling at all. I remember that everybody was in high spirits, everybody laughing and talking and visiting with folks they hadn't seen for a long time. A right jolly day. I was a-worrying about something else though. I was wondering where on earth the preacher was. We had Uncle Ira Combs, that married Ma and Dad, contracted to come, but the day got longer, dinner got all on the table ready to be eaten, and still no Uncle Ira. I was all dressed up in my wedding clothes and getting so nervous I thought I'd go out of my head. We were supposed to be leaving on the down train for Lexington on our honeymoon, and it wasn't too long to traintime.

'Finally, when I was about ready to burst out crying, some of the men rode down to find out about the preacher. Turned out someone was dying and Uncle Ira had to stay by the bedside. So the men searched around and the only preacher they could find free was Alonzo Fields grubbing in his new-ground. Said he said, "Why, I can't come to no wedding. I'm a-grubbing!" They had to just beg him to come, and then he wanted to wash and put on clean clothes. "No time for fuss and frills," they told him. "These people have to get married and catch their train." So they got him right out of his field, and he stood up all sweaty and dirty in the middle of all the fine dresses and read the marriage words.

'After he pronounced us man and wife, everybody was kind of quiet a little while, like there was something else to happen, it was all over so quick. Finally someone said, "Why, there ought to be some kind of music!" Well, we hadn't thought of that, but all big weddings do have some kind of music, don't they? Up spoke Jewel — she and Pauline were the two least ones then — "Me and Pauline will sing. We know a song about 'There Was an Old Woman and She Had a Little Pig.' We know it all the way through!" Everybody laughed then and Mrs. Zande said she thought that was a fine song, and all said they'd like to hear it sung, so Jewel and Pauline, dressed just alike in new little blue-checked gingham dresses, stood over under the snowball bush and sang. Their red hair shone in the sun and their cheeks blushed from being bashful. They started out brave and loud, got littler and lower as they went along, almost stopped but Mrs. Zande got to humming along with them and so they finished it.

> There was an old woman and she had a little pig,
> > Mmm-mmm-mmm.
> There was an old woman and she had a little pig,
> > Mmm-mmm-mmm.
> There was an old woman and she had a little pig,
> Didn't cost much cause it wasn't very big,
> > Mmm-mmm-mmm.
>
> Now this old woman kept the pig in the barn,

Mmm-mmm-mmm.
Now this old woman kept the pig in the barn,
Mmm-mmm-mmm.
Now this old woman kept the pig in the barn,
Prettiest little thing she had on the farm,
Mmm-mmm-mmm.

Now this old woman fed the pig on clover,
Mmm-mmm-mmm.
Now this old woman fed the pig on clover,
Mmm-mmm-mmm.
Now this old woman fed the pig on clover,
It laid down and died all over,
Mmm-mmm-mmm.

The little piggy died cause it couldn't get its breath,
Mmm-mmm-mmm.

The little piggy died cause it couldn't get its breath,
    Mmm-mmm-mmm.
The little piggy died cause it couldn't get its breath,
Wasn't that an awful death?
    Mmm-mmm-mmm.

The little old woman she died of grief,
    Mmm-mmm-mmm.
The little old woman she died of grief,
    Mmm-mmm-mmm.
The little old woman she died of grief,
Wasn't that a sad relief?
    Mmm-mmm-mmm.

The little old man he sobbed and sighed,
    Mmm-mmm-mmm.
The little old man he sobbed and sighed,
    Mmm-mmm-mmm.
The little old man he sobbed and sighed,
Then he too laid down and died,
    Mmm-mmm-mmm.

Now that was the end of the one, two, three,
    Mmm-mmm-mmm.
Now that was the end of the one, two, three,
    Mmm-mmm-mmm.
Now that was the end of the one, two, three,
The man and the woman and the little pig-ee,
    Mmm-mmm-mmm.

The good old book lies on the shelf,
    Mmm-mmm-mmm.
The good old book lies on the shelf,
    Mmm-mmm-mmm.

The good old book lies on the shelf,
If you want any more you can sing it yourself,
Mmm-mmm-mmm.

'Then everybody clapped their hands, and wanted the girls to sing some more, but they said that was all they knew. Mrs. Zande said why didn't everybody sing "John Riley" — she knew that was my favorite ballad, and so she started in and we all joined her, I did too, and Leon, singing at our own wedding!

As I walked out one summer's morning to take the cool and pleasant air, I spied a fair and most beauti-ful dam-sel, her cheeks were like some li-ly fair.

As I walked out one summer's morning
To take the cool and pleasant air,
I spied a fair and most beautiful damsel
Her cheeks were like some lily fair.

Then I walked up to her a-saying,
Don't you want to be a sailor's wife?
O no, O no, she quickly answered,
My mind is to lead a single life.

Kind miss, kind miss, what makes you different
From all the rest of womankind?
You are so fair, so young and handsome,
My heart to you in love inclines.

Kind sir, kind sir, I could have married
Some two or three long years ago
All to a man that they call John Riley,
He was the cause of my overthrow.

O come leave off thinking of John Riley
And sail with me to some distant shore,
We'll go over to old Pennsylvanie
And there we'll live forevermore.

No, I won't leave off thinking of John Riley
Nor sail with you to no distant shore,
My mind is with him, I can never forsake him
Although his face I may never see no more.

Then I walked up to her with sweet kisses,
And the kisses I gave her was one, two, three,
Saying I am the man that they call John Riley
Returning home to marry thee.

'You know, that was like — well, I had always liked the song, but it got to be my favorite after Leon came back to Pine Mountain after the war — he had to go — and kept on until he got me to liking him. John Riley seemed to fit, somehow.

'I have to laugh now about Dad's remark about marrying foreigners. There's Unie married to Tom, from India, and Pauline to Paul, born in Czechoslovakia. And he thinks a lot of his furrin sons-in-law now, don't he? I guess it was a good thing I made a start for the others!'

That was May's story and her telling of it made me almost jealous that I wasn't there, which was impossible because I was several years away from being born then. Still, the story made such an impression on me that to this day I think of that wedding scene when I hear 'John Riley' or 'Old Woman Had a Little Pig.' It's curious how songs will take on meanings that don't really belong to them like that. Like 'Twilight A-Stealing' always makes me think of my sore toe, and sometimes yet I can feel a twinge in that toe whenever I hear that tune. And I know a lullaby that near breaks my heart, because to me it means the sadness of death.

Being Patty's sister always did make me feel stuck-up, and I wasn't the only one, we were all of us proud of Patty. She knew just exactly what to do and say all the time, could stand right up and talk with anyone on earth. She was slender and pretty, had dark red hair and Dad's brown eyes, and when she put on a dress it looked three times as good as it did on anyone else. Patty had an *air*, the boys followed her around all the time, and she didn't yet lack for girl friends. What she said mattered to everybody. She kept a sassy tongue in her head, and everyone said she was like Granny Katty there, but somehow you were pleased to be bawled out by Patty. It made you feel important. And when she wasn't being sassy she was laughing and joking and doing something nice for someone, going to see Granny and taking her some fish, because she knew that was Granny's best liking; bringing me hair ribbons and letting me use her face powder.

Patty loved the beauty of our mountains with a great tenderness. To us she never melted and talked soft, from the inside out, but I remember once I was walking down from the cornfield with Patty, and all of a sudden she stopped and got a long quivery breath and I looked up at her. Thought she was getting a pain in her side, like she sometimes did. But she was just looking far off along the tops of the ridges that dwindled down and down to the river far below us. She had the softest, dreamiest smile on her lips and her eyes were so dark and deep. Then she looked down quick at me, stern again, like I had caught her in some meanness or other.

'Look! Look at the hills! Tell me, do you see them? Do you ever *look* and see them?' Her eyes got soft again. 'See, it's a fall day today, yonder is a ridge almost all turned red and yellow, and that one's yellow and brown and green, and that purple haze and that gold sunlight, look how it makes them so soft and glowy. And that sky, the color of a robin's egg exactly. Stand and look up, you can't see to the bottom of the sky, blue-greeny and clear as the branch water. It looks so new and young; I think that must be the newest thing in this world, the last thing the Lord made. His little baby. You know, here is why I don't like to go to church in the church-house. Seems to me like if you want to find God, He'll be right here.'

It kind of scared me a little, hearing Patty talk like that, but I knew just what she meant. It flew to my mind then what I had heard a girl say once, a girl that had come home with Patty and Edna from Berea College. She said, 'I never saw a sunset until I met Patty Ritchie.'

Then Patty got married, and I saw that she loved her own little family with the same complete tenderness she had shown that day when she talked of the hills.

When Winkie was born, that was a hard time in our house. Patty had high blood, the doctor said, and that was pretty bad to cause trouble. Then when she was seven months along they came up from Hazard and told Mom that Patty was in the hospital bad off. I hung around and tried to hear but nobody was thinking of me then. I heard them say something like one convulsion right after another, and the words didn't mean anything to me. But their faces and their low speeches did. My heart got like something had laid hold of it and turned it to cold stone in my breast. Never before had I felt such fearful dread. When Grandpa Hall had died I had not felt at all that way. Grandpa Hall was an old man and he never did pay me much mind; I liked him and he liked me and still he was a stranger to me. Then one day Mallie said to me, 'Jean, run out to Ollie's and tell her Grandpa Hall is dead.' I could hear Mom crying out loud in the house and I wondered why everybody took on so whenever someone died. I had not been to many funerals and it was mostly all a big curiosity to me, like I guess it is to all little children. Well, I got out to Ollie's and told them, and I got Helen out and asked her if she thought we ought to cry at the funeral. Helen said she didn't know, but she thought maybe we should, him being our own grandpa. I said I was afraid something would happen and maybe I couldn't cry and Helen said well, she thought she would cry whether I did or not. They preached Grandpa's funeral in his front yard, everybody in dark clothes sitting around on chairs and home-made benches set up in a half-circle around the coffin. The women fanned and cried into their handkerchiefs, and even the men sniffed and wiped their eyes sometimes. I could just see the tip of Grandpa's nose, and as the second and then the third preacher shouted on and on, I thought, 'Maybe if I saw all of Grandpa's face I could cry like the rest.' Finally the preachers said they'd finish up at the grave, with prayer and song, and so the men gathered around and bore Grandpa's coffin on their shoulders up through Uncle Lee's pasture, and all the people followed behind, winding around the narrow gravelly path, by the haw tree and across the gullies and among the pawpaw bushes, up the steep pasture hill to the graveyard.

They set the coffin down and made prayer and sang some more, then the time came when they opened up the coffin and we all marched by Grandpa lying there all white. All the women started to scream and wave their arms, looked to me like they were going crazy. All I could do was stand there and watch. I couldn't squeeze out a single tear.

That had been the last time I had thought much about dying, and at that time I had been mostly concerned about my own self, with not being able to appear properly sorrowful about Grandpa. But now the thought of death was terribly different. All manner of thoughts passed through my mind while they talked about Patty, thoughts about Heaven and Hell, and bury-ings and what happened to you under the ground, and I don't know what all now. And I couldn't make sense out of any of those things happening to Patty; she belonged right here in the hills she loved so, and God wouldn't take her away.

When evening came they took Mom and some of the older girls off to Hazard with them. Toward morning they brought her back again and she went to bed for most of the day. She said

Patty hadn't taken a turn yet. Then someone came and said Patty was worse. Mom said someone had to milk the old cow and she got the buckets and went up to the barn. Dad followed her and they stayed and stayed. Dad brought the milk back and said Mom had stayed to salt the cow.

Then in came Truman with a big grin on his face, and he said Patty had a little boy, that he favored a little bitty doll, no bigger, that they had him in an incubator, that Patty was resting fine and feeling so much better they had sent him home to say not to worry.

Everybody began jumping up and laughing, Mallie flew to put supper on the table, but I shot off through the pawpaw patch to the barn. I came up to Mom and she was sitting on the milking stool stripping the cream from the heifer, and she had her face sort of buried in the cow's flank. I touched her on the shoulder and she looked up at me and her face had a world of trouble in it. I told her. She got up and poured the cream out of the cup into her bucket. She started to say something and couldn't. She stood there looking at me in a blank way.

'Well, I thank you, Lord,' she said at last.

Winkie was a funny-looking little thing for the longest time, tiny and scraggly and wrinkled up, had a face for all the world like a little monkey. Everybody, all the women round, said they thought he had the poorest chance of any child they ever saw. Patty and Bill would laugh whenever anyone came in to see the baby, said they were almost ashamed to show him off to anyone. But that was a pure show, that little thing, and every soul that saw him said, 'He's a lively one, and listen to him squall, you'll see in a month or two.' But Winkie weighed only a little bit over two pounds, and a lot of folks said he didn't have but one chance in a hundred to live and grow up.

Well, he stayed puny like that, long and thin, until he was about four months old. Then, bang, all of a sudden he was a fat dumpling with rosy cheeks and light curly hair, deep dimples and a smile like Patty's. She said he was a Reynolds in his actions though, pure deviltry sparkling out of his blue eyes, but I think she said 'deviltry' just to tease Bill. Winkie was just lively.

Never was a child so lovely, or so full of life, or so petted. He had us all twined right around his little fat pink fingers and he sure did know that too. He was the quickest thing to learn, seemed like in no time he was doing all the tricks the other children took a year and sometimes two to be doing — saying sweet little words, throwing kisses, playing hide-and-go-seek, standing alone, standing on his head and peeping back through his legs.

Bill, his daddy, he thought a sight in this world of his boy. Mom and Dad would shake their heads and say, 'I don't reckon I ever saw a man make so over a young un.' The child would just dart into his daddy's sight and Bill would start to grin and brag and ask everybody, 'Did you ever see the likes of that?'

And Patty was just as bad as Bill was. Oftentimes I was by when she stripped him off to give him his bath. He'd sit there on her knee by the warm kitchen stove, be cooing and twinkling, and she'd just stop washing and look at him funny.

'Now who can tell me where you did come from? I want to know, that's all, I just like to know. You're too good for this world and too full of meanness to come from Heaven!

'I know and you can't fool me. You're a little silly star, the brightest one, fell out of the sky one night.'

Then he'd gaze up solemn into her face and she'd say, soft, 'No, no, you're a pure angel from Heaven . . . and why did I get picked out to have your keeping? Your Mommy and your Daddy, they're just common people and God gives us an angel for a child. Sweetest, sweetest, how can you be . . . how can you *be?*'

And she'd snatch him into her arms and cry, 'God love! God love my baby, bless its looks, my dirty angel-baby. Mommy can't stand it she loves you so!' And she'd hug Winkie up so tight that he'd start sometimes to cry from the pain.

Dad would say, over and over in the day, about his work, 'That shore is a master boy! The master'st young un I ever seed.' That's the way we all felt about Winkie.

He started to walk before he was nine months old, and from then on his quick little feet were never still, only in sleep. You could hear them running here, running there, in the door, out the door, up the steps, down the walk, through the rooms, running, running, laughing his bubbling laugh and talking his sweet important little talk.

After dinner, soon past noon, the little feet would run up to his Mommy and there stop. Hands reach up.

'Mommy. Mommy, tell me a story and sing me a song!'

And Patty would pick him up and hug him and kiss him and they would settle cozy in the rocking chair. He would throw both arms around her neck and be all sleepy and soft.

'Well,' Patty would begin, 'once upon a time there was a good, pretty little man no bigger than your thumb . . .'

'And what was his name? And what was his name? His name?'

'. . . and his name was — WEE WILLIE WINKIE!'

'. . . Me! Me! Me!'

'. . . and he wore a long white . . .'

'Nighty-gown!'

'And every night bout dark, Wee Willie Winkie would take a big tall red candle, and go . . .'

'Running, running, running through the town . . .'

'Peeping through the . . .'

'Window . . .'

'Calling through the . . .'

'Lock . . .'

'Are the children in their . . .'

'Beds it's past eight o'clock! Now sing me a song, Mommy.'

'And what'll I sing?'

'Sing a song. Sing a song, sing the horsey song.'

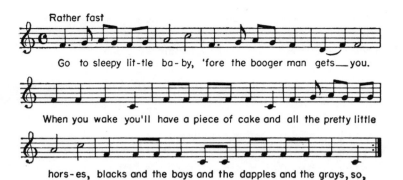

Rather fast

Go to sleepy lit-tle ba-by, 'fore the booger man gets—you.

When you wake you'll have a piece of cake and all the pretty little

hors-es, blacks and the boys and the dapples and the grays, so,

Go to sleepy little baby
Fore the booger-man gets you!
When you wake you'll have a piece of cake
And all the pretty little horses,
      Blacks and the bays
        And the dapples and the grays — so

Go to sleepy little baby
Fore the booger-man gets you!

Go to sleepy little baby
Fore the booger-man gets you!
When you wake you'll have a piece of cake
And a coach and four little ponies —
      A black and a bay
        And a dapple and a gray — so

Go to sleepy little baby
Fore the booger-man gets you!

The rest of the story is the hardest thing I ever tried to tell; I don't think I ever have told it in words, out loud, and I don't guess I ever will.

It was on a Saturday in the early fall, a high windy day. The leaves spun down from the trees and then swirled up again in a gay dizzy dance. Bill brought Winkie up from Hazard where they lived to stay the day with us, because Patty was washing and he wouldn't get two feet away from her. I remember everybody was tickled to death to see him, especially Raymond's children, but I couldn't stay to play with them then because some of us were going to town and it was bustime, so we ran off down the branch. All the way down to the big road we could hear the children's voices on the wind, Winkie and Paul and Joey and Judy, running about and calling to one another. It was such a day.

We hurried with our buying and got the very next bus back, up the steps and into the house and no one was there. I had got some pretty dress goods and wanted to show it to Mom and Mallie so I looked around for them. Out behind the house and around Raymond's house, and there they all were, sitting and standing around on the rockwall by the road. Looked to me like they were talking and laughing, and I ran up to Mom, said look what I got, and she looked at me and broke out crying. I don't know why it is, when you start to say a thing, and whoever you're saying it to looks at you and starts in crying, why you're just bound to say the thing you started to, funny or sad. So I was still laughing and reaching out my dress goods to Mom. 'Looky, red flowers and I can't wear red! Think it's pretty? What's the matter?'

Alma, Raymond's wife, said, 'Hush. Winkie got hurt.'

They told us then that the children had been playing like children will, catching the leaves and playing like they themselves were leaves too, then they were the wind and ran around blowing the leaves to make them dance. And all, all forever running after Winkie because his little legs wouldn't let him be still and the others could never really keep up to him. Then Paul looked down the branch and hollered, 'Here comes Daddy, Daddy's coming home! Come on, he'll let us ride up the branch!' Raymond's three, because they were older, got to the old Ford first and he slowed her down until they climbed onto the running board. Winkie came running behind the car, running, running so hard trying to catch up, and Raymond didn't even know he was there.

Then he did catch up. Mom said she could see him laughing and patting the car sides, reaching up trying to get a hold of something to pull up by, and her hol'*ring every breath telling him to stop, telling Raymond to stop, but not a one of them heard her. Raymond stepped on the gas to get up a little speed and the car slipped sideways, just a little, in the muddy road. He said that not until he had gone on ever so far did he or the children see little Winkie lying muddy and still where the big hind tire rolled over his chest.

Mom says it is a sight she will all of her life see, in the dead of night when things come back to you, the two little legs, so quick and live, running, running, taking him laughing to his little death.

Everybody flew to him, and they picked him up and laid him on the seat of the car with his head on Kitty's lap. Seemed like Kitty was ever the one when trouble got us. Raymond couldn't do a thing, much less drive, and Bill drove down to the hospital quicker than anyone ever did make that distance.

When the rest of us got to the hospital, they had put Winkie in a crib with a hard board for a mattress. Whenever he got his breath it sounded like he had the whooping cough. Patty was sitting in a chair by him and she had a hold of his hand, just sitting there, looking at him. Seemed like she couldn't catch on to what had happened. She had on her apron where she had been washing. It was wet over her stomach, and there were soap-suds still sticking to her arms above the elbows. She would talk whenever anybody came up to her, but she'd still talk whenever they went away.

'I don't see why they have give him such a hard bed, he likes a soft bed, he likes a featherbed. You know, my baby will cry when he wakes on a hard bed . . . a soft bed . . . a feather-bed. He wants me to rock him . . . I know he wants Mommy to rock him . . . did Winkie take his nap today? Did you take your little nap? My baby's sick, why won't the doctor come?

Go bring a nurse, get some medicine . . . he wants a soft bed. Why won't you let me hold my little boy-baby in my arms?'

They said one doctor had examined Winkie, and that he wanted to get another one to look at him. Said there was nothing wrong with him that you could see, maybe inside . . . nobody was supposed to move him, take him up . . . Then the doctor went away, back down the stairs, nobody knows where.

Once in a while a spry little nurse would come in, clicking her heels. She'd look at Winkie and feel his pulse and chew her chewing-gum, then she'd say in a bright happy voice, 'Don't you all worry now, doc'll be here real soon and we'll be able to tell you more about it. The child's probably not too bad hurt. Now, you remember, Miz Reynolds honey, don't you pick him up or anything.' She'd give Patty a brisk pat on the head and smile around at us all, and trip away.

Once when I went off down the hall to get a drink I could hear her around the corner, I guess she was talking into the telephone.

'Say, Doctor, I don't like to bother you again like this, but you see this baby . . . Yes I know it's your day . . . Yes, but I think the baby is . . . Yes that's the one, the Reynolds boy . . . Yes Doctor . . . No Doctor . . . Oh, I wouldn't think of calling you except . . . Tell them what? . . . Well, honest, I think I'd come if I's you . . . Half an hour? . . . Oh, that's swell Doctor . . . I'll go right in and tell them . . . Yes . . . Good-by!'

By and by the doctor did come, and very business-like he did look, not speaking to anyone much. But when he saw Winkie and Patty there he got different and very gentle speaking, and then he made her go away and he bent over the bed for a long time. Then he lifted the baby up and laid him in his mother's arms. 'You go ahead and rock him if you want to, it'll be all right.' And the doctor went away, down the stairs and out the door. He said he'd come back again soon.

Patty sat in the rocking chair and rocked. Winkie whimpered after a while and opened his eyes and we crowded around the door. Something or other made us stay outside and not go in there, all of us but Bill. But he belonged. It was like, well, like holy ground.

Now Patty was more herself, and she knew. I could tell by the looks of her face, like someone had hit her, and she was just looking around to see how it was, all shocked and surprised. For a minute she looked mad like she wanted to hit back, then Winkie woke up and her face just crumbled down to him.

He began to move himself around a little on her lap and that gave us hope. Someone said, thank God he wasn't paralyzed.

'Mommy, my head hurts me, Mommy.' Patty smoothed and kissed his curls and she began to cry without any tears, and she tried to talk to him.

'Tell Mommy about it, my angel one. Tell Mommy where it hurts you. Mommy will kiss it and make it well, you tell Mommy. Oh, Mommy's pretty little man, golden hair, eyes of blue, you love me and . . .'

'I love you . . . Mommy I think my belly hurts me too . . . kiss, kiss to make it well . . .'

And so they rocked and rocked and said little lovey words to each other. At last he got his little arms up around her neck in their old way. It must have strained him in his sore and bruised body for he began to cry a little more. We were all still as stone.

'Mommy, I sleepy . . . I hurt . . . I sleepy . . . Mommy tell me a story and sing me a song.'

That has been the pitifullest thing in all of my life, those two hurting voices trying to tell that gay little story. Winkie whimpering on some of the words and some of them you couldn't hear because of his great breathing. Patty's voice was low and raspy and every word she spoke seemed to tear her heart out, but the tenderness came through the hard sound of it, and the loving.

Then Winkie said sing the horsey song, and he went peacefully to sleep just like he always did, seemed like he didn't hear his Mommy crying as she sang.

> Go to sleepy little baby
> Fore the booger-man gets you!
> When you wake you'll have a piece of cake
> And all the pretty little horses,
> > Blacks and the bays
> > And the dapples and the grays — so
> Go to sleepy little baby
> Fore the booger-man gets you!

Patty and Bill said they didn't want to live without children, and the doctor told Patty she most likely would not live if she did have another baby. She never really stopped grieving for Winkie, and finally the next year in the fall when her second little boy was born early, and dead, she died too, and they buried them both in the same coffin, the little baby in her arms. Some talked about that, said it was wrong and an unnatural thing to do, but we all wanted it that way. It was the least we could do, to let Patty carry her own boy-baby through the big strange gates of Paradise.

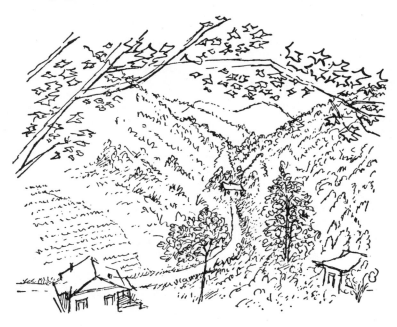

CHAPTER THIRTEEN

The ways of the world are a-coming — up Cyarr!
Biled shirts and neckties,
Powder-pots and veils,
Pizen fotched-on liquor,
Doctor-pills, and ails —
Hit's a sight, all the brash that's a-coming — up Cyarr! *

IT IS a pretty common notion that we in the Kentucky mountains live and do things differently from everybody else
in the world, that we are old-fashioned in our ways and somehow quaint and queer, that we've not changed much since we
came in from the old countries of England, Scotland, and
Ireland. At least that was the notion folks from the level country
held about us until just a few years back, and some hold it still.

* 'Up Carr Creek,' from *Kinfolks*, by Ann Cobb, Courier-Journal Job
Printing Company, Louisville, Kentucky.

Well, it's partly true and partly not. It's true that it was a hard matter for us to do much traveling, rough creek roads and eternal mountains to cross before we could get anywhere. So we stayed home and lived out our lives in a peaceful way, we didn't bother anyone, and it was a good kind of life. Still, whenever visitors from the level land came into our parts, we'd always treat them as well as we knew how, take them in off the roads and put them up for the nights. And it was a wonder to us to hear them tell about the places they came from, where roads were smooth as a floor and water was piped right into the houses, and all kinds of new ways like that. Then they'd likely ask us to sing some of our songs for them, and we'd maybe get to telling hant tales before the night was over. We'd sit and listen and wonder if it'd ever be so we could get out to any of those foreign places. We never thought that these same new ways would ever start up around where we lived.

I guess the biggest changes took place before I was born, except for the radio. The settlement schools first and then the railroad, they began to bring the ways of the world to us in a kind of steady trickle, so that when I came along we were already seeing many new ways. The big thing that the settlement schools did was to bring in level-country people who settled among us and whose ways of doing things, whose very speech and actions, helped us to see that there was a different kind of life than the hard one we knew. In my family they tell how the settlement schools got started in our hills.

One day in the late spring of 1895 a strange woman drove into Hazard in a wagon, said she had come all the way from Lexington down in the Blue Grass country. That was when the railroad had got as far along as Jackson over in Breathitt County. This woman said she had traveled on that new railroad train to Jackson all the way from Lexington in one day, then it took her two days to get the forty miles on to Hazard with the wagon and team. Her name was Katherine Pettit and folks couldn't rightly make out why she had come all that weary way up into Perry County, she had no people here that anyone could see. But she was a friendly and a nice-spoken woman, and she had a right good turn and people she'd meet up with would be talking away with her in no time. Some said she was a little bit nosey, but most liked her all the same for that. She was eternally asking questions about everything in under the sun and she always got answered, especially from the womenfolks. They told her all she wanted to know about the war just over, the French-Eversole fight, that was. The last feuding man was shot in March of that year.

I guess there were about five hundred people living in Hazard at that time, and that woman went visiting nearly every one of them, talking with the women and girls and staying all night with them. They said for all she was such a lady and from so far away, she would pitch in and help do, just like she was one of the family, and sometimes she'd come right out and rail at them over some little thing they were doing, maybe sweeping the floors, she'd say they were doing it in a wrong way or a hard way, and she'd take the broom and show a better way of sweeping. Few women would usually have stood for the likes of that, but Miss Pettit had such a way about her that she got by with it.

She stayed around for a while like that, among the people, then she went away home. But for several years after that, every summer when the corn was about knee-high, Miss Pettit would roll in from Lexington. They said other women got to coming with her, said they'd bring flower seeds and little tricks for the folks. People got to looking for them every year. The women couldn't wait to see what kind of pretty clothes the visiting women would have *this* year.

1899 it was, for it has been noted down, a strange thing happened. The women came into Hazard, and what did they do but pitch a tent under a clump of trees right in town, drive off the pigs and cows and chickens, and start teaching school! Yes, they put up the flag and a lot of bright pretty pictures, and they had brought in a dozen or so little red and yellow and blue chairs to suit the size of little folks. There were about five of the women teaching the classes, and funny classes they were. How to cook, sew, mend, and darn, how to take care of sick folks. Every day they read the Bible and talked about the evils of drink. Best of all they had a lot of singing and play-games. And they tell that before hardly any time at all that school was fuller of grown girls and women, and big overgrown boys than it was with young uns, and the Women, as everyone got to call them, never turned anyone away.

Our family lived over in Knott County then, up on Clear Creek, but the news of the tent school in Hazard got over there fast. Great-granddad Solomon, Granny Katty's daddy, lived over on the Forks-of-Troublesome, over twenty miles away, and one day he went over to see the goings-on for himself. A woman named Lucy Furman, who later wrote some books about our country there and the settlement schools, noted down about Granddaddy Solomon going to see the tent, and what he said:

A visitor of the late summer was a beautiful old man with a shock of white hair, wearing a crimson linsey hunting-shirt and linen trousers, who, after sitting silent all day, watching the doings, said, 'Women, my name is Solomon Everidge. Sence I was a leetle shirt-tail boy hoe-ing corn on the steep mountainsides, I have looked up Troublesome, and down Troublesome, for somebody to come in and larn us something. My childhood passed, then my manhood, now I am old and my head is a-blooming for the grave, and still nobody hain't come. I growed up ignorant and mean; my offsprings was wuss; my grands is wusser, squandering their time drinking and shooting; and what my greats will be if something hain't done to stop the meanness of their maneuvers, God only knows!

'When I heard the tale of you Women, I walked the twenty-four mile acrost the ridges to sarch out hit's truth. I am persuaded you air the ones I have looked for all my lifetime. Come over on Troublesome, Women, and do for us what you air a-doing here.'

So, the tale goes, the next summer the Women went over to Hindman on the Forks-of-Troublesome, and they put their tents up on the hillside there. It was a sight to see how the young and the old and the growing came gathering in there. Granddaddy Solomon was the proudest. He said it did his old eyes good to see big boys like his grandsons and their friends sitting peaceable on the green hillside hemming handkerchiefs and guarding the school and the Women, instead of running wild up and down the creek, riding the horses to death and drinking and shooting up the towns.

Granddad Solomon and the other men around Hindman got together and decided they wanted the Women to stay and never leave, so they donated land and logs among them, and all pitched in and built the Hindman Settlement School, and there she stands today. Newspapers from off said it was the first settlement school ever built or even thought of, out in the country like that. Well, when Miss Pettit got the school to running smooth, she went to Pine Mountain in Harlan County where they had been begging her to come and start up a school. In 1913 she began work on the Pine Mountain Settlement School. If you go down there right now, anyone will tell you that these are two of the finest schools to be found anywhere in the Kentucky Mountains. They always have been.

Our home in Perry County was halfway between the two schools, some miles closer to Hindman, but Dad sent some of his children to one and some to the other, as they got old enough. My brother Wilmer and I, though, we always felt somehow cheated out of our rights because just at the time we got to high-school age, Perry County built us a high school in Viper, and we didn't get to leave home for another four years, and missed the settlement schools all around. I especially had been dreaming and thinking of going off to one or the other of the schools for many a year, ever since I was big enough to listen to the others talk. Mallie told me the oldest story about it, for she remembers the very first day any of the family ever had anything to do with the School. It was the

Hindman School, and Mallie and Unie were the ones.

'Why, I guess one main reason Dad moved us over from Clear Creek to Hindman when he did was so that he could send us children to the Settlement School.

'One day about a week before time for school to open, Mom decided we ought to go see the Women. She picked out Unie and me, being we were about middle-ways the family then, eight or ten years old we were. So she thought we'd be the best ones to represent all the others. I recollect she said to us, "We're new moved around here, and it won't do no harm for you all to go up and see the Women and say howdy and tell them you and your brother and sisters'll be coming to the school next week, when they open her up. You want them to like you."

'She dressed us up in our new pink dresses she'd made us for school. I remember I thought they were the prettiest dresses — pink calico with wide skirts and ruffles at the neck. She worked a long time taking down our braids and brushing our long red hair loose and wavy. She tied it back with ribbons and it hung down to our waists in the back. Then she sent us to the woods to gather some wildflowers. "I hear that if you want to please them Women plum to death, just take them wildflowers, so you stop on the way and pick them two nice big bunches. And remember that you are Ritchies, and speak up nice and act proper."

'We started out, all pink and starched and feeling so important. We gathered our arms clear full and running over with all manner of pretty wood flowers and leaves and we marched up to the door where the Women lived. I was getting a little shaky by this time but I knew Unie'd do enough talking for us both. And she usually did, too. Not that she was show-offy or anything; seemed like she just knew what to say and who to say it to and when to say it. And she could tell when it was the best thing to keep her mouth shut, too. I don't know, it's a gift I guess, and used to be I'd have given anything to be like her. Oh, she wasn't sassy, now, it wasn't that. She got scared of strangers same as any of us, but she'd not give up and put her finger in her mouth. She'd get a long breath and r'ar back and talk to them as sensible as a grown person, might near. She sure was smart.

'Well, anyway we knocked and a pretty, smiley woman opened the door. May Stone it was, and I don't think I had ever seen anyone so stylish before. We said howdy and she asked us to come right in and we all went into the parlor and sat on the pretty chairs. Miss Pettit came in then and we gave them our flowers. Seemed to tickle them a right smart.

'The one who opened the door for us said, "My name is May Stone and this is Katherine Pettit. What are your names? I don't think we have seen you before."

'Unie and I we were busy taking in everything about the room, and the women's dresses, and the nice way they talked, to tell the others. But seemed like that was all I could do, was look, the cat had my tongue for a fact. I punched Unie and she punched me, with our elbows, then she looked right at May Stone and smiled.

' "We are Balis Ritchie's girls. This one is Mallie and I'm named Unie. May and Ollie are older'n us, and Raymond our little brother, he's school age too, but not Kitty. She's the baby. We are coming to the school next week and Mommie said — and we thought it'd be a nice thing to come and say howdy, and see if it was all right."

'I was so proud of Unie right then. Gee-oh, if I could talk like that! And the Women acted like they were pleased too. They laughed and asked us a whole lot of questions and all that we said seemed to suit them fine. Specially when they learned that Solomon Everidge was our great-granddaddy. When we started home the Women hugged us, said they thought we'd be a credit to the school!

'They were so pretty and sweet, yet so natural and good, my heart like to burst. What if I could grow up to be like that! Folks said they could hoe corn and wash and scrub too, and still they were so — gee-oh, no one knows how happy me and Unie were going home. It was like the whole world was opening up like a blossom.'

If it hadn't been for the settlement schools, many of the old mountain songs would have died out when the ways of the world came in on us. But the Women loved our music and plays, so that they became a regular part of the life around the two schools. Every new girl or boy that'd come in, the Women'd soon find out what ballads she or he knew, and that song'd be written down and taught to all the other children. My sister May sang them one at Pine Mountain that they put into a little book they used to sing out of. Her song was the Bible story of Mary and Martha and Lazarus, called 'The Little Family.'

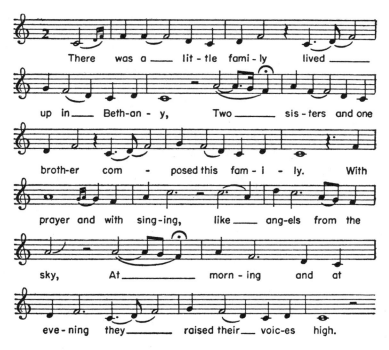

There was a little family lived up in Bethany
Two sisters and one brother composed this family.

With prayer and with singing like angels from the sky,
At morning and at evening they raised their voices high.

They lived in peace and pleasure for many a lonely year,
And laid away their treasures beyond this vale of tears.

Though poor and without money, their kindness made
    amends;
Their house was ever open to Jesus and His friends.

Although they lived so happy, so kind, so pure and good,
Their brother was afflicted, and by it thrown in bed.
Poor Martha and her sister, they wept aloud and cried,
But still he grew no better; he lingered on and died.

The Jews came to the sisters, laid Lazarus in the tomb,
And tried for to comfort and drive away their gloom.
When Jesus heard the tidings, far in a distant land,
So swiftly did He travel to join that lonely band.

And while He was a-coming, Martha met him on the way,
And told Him that her brother had died and passed away;
He blessed and he cheered her, and told her not to weep,
For in Him was the power to raise him from his sleep.

And while He was a-coming, Mary met Him, lonely too,
Down at His feet a-weeping, rehearsed the tale of woe.
When Jesus saw her weeping, He fell a-weeping too,
And wept until they showed Him where Lazarus lay en-
    tombed.

He rolled away the cover and looked upon the grave,
And prayed unto His Father His loving friend to save;
And Lazarus in full power came from that gloomy mound,
And in full life and vigor he walked upon the ground.

Come all ye who love Jesus, and do His holy will,
Like Mary and like Martha, He'll always use you well;

He'll comfort and redeem you and take you to the skies,
And bid you live forever where pleasure never dies.

Then there was 'Aunt Sal's Song.' Aunt Sal and Uncle William Creech's cabin was close by the school on the Pine Mountain. They gave land for the school and lumber for the buildings and were of help in many ways, and everybody called them Aunt Sal and Uncle William. Aunt Sal's song is the only one anyone ever heard her sing in her lifetime, and they called it 'Aunt Sal's Song' for so long a time that now it has no other name but that. I always thought it was a funny song, but the boys around home never did.

(Arrangement copyright 1953 by BMI)

> A gentleman came to our house,
> He did not tell his name;
> I knew he came a-courting
> Although he were ashame,
> > O, although he were ashame.
>
> He hitched his chair up to my side,
> His fancy pleased me well;
> I thought the spirit moved him
> Some handsome tale to tell,
> > O, some handsome tale to tell.

But there he sat the livelong night
And never a word did say,
With many a sigh and bitter groan
He ofttimes wished for day,
    O, he ofttimes wished for day.

The chickens they began to crow
And daylight did appear,
How do you do, good morning sir,
I'm glad to see you here,
    O, I'm glad to see you here.

He was weary all the livelong night,
He was weary all of his life,
If this is what you call courting, boys,
I'll never take a wife,
    No, I'll never take a wife.

Now when he goes in company
The girls all laugh for sport,
Saying, yonder goes that ding-dang fool
That don't know how to court.
    O, that don't know how to court.

By the time I was old enough to sing, most of the others were going to the Pine Mountain School, and I used to get mad because it took them all away from home and left me trudging along to grade school in Viper. The oldest ones were through the Hindman School then, and were off to college or married, but the time I remember best was when Patty, Edna, Jewel, and Pauline were in Pine Mountain all together. It sure was a happy day whenever their letter would come from the Post Office telling the day they'd be coming home for the summertime. Dad would whistle and hum and sharpen up all the hoes on the place. 'Plenty of work hands now, and in good time too!' Mom would raise up and say what about the garden patch, she managed that, and she was making her own plans for when the girls got home. Mallie would be sorting buttons and thread and studying patterns for next year's school dresses for the girls. As for me, every time I'd wash the dishes I'd think with a lifting heart that soon the house would be full of noise and people again and I could go back to being the baby and never have to wash all the old dishes alone again. It was like looking for Christmas, almost, it was such a happy time.

One such homecoming I remember in particular. It was dogwood winter and the rain had been coming down for three days hand running. Worry filled our house. The girls had started from school two days ago, so their letter said, and it was a long walk, some forty miles through the mountain trails. It was a hard enough trip in good weather, but the storm could bring real danger. Flooded creekbed paths, falling timber, landslides in the parts of the road that had been worked recently. On top of that, the walking in the bitter cold rain for two days could bring on dreaded flu or pneumonia. Mom allowed they hadn't started yet. Her children knew enough not to go a long trip in a stormy time. But Dad thought different.

'I know my girls wants to get home, now, and like's not it wasn't raining when they started out. Once they start for home, I don't care where from, they won't stop nor turn back for Hell or high water.'

The third day came on wet as ever, and the black noon time turned into blacker evening and still that gray rain poured hard. On our tin roof it sounded ten times harder. Any other time it was a dreamy, singing sound, and many's the time I have gone to sleep to that rain lullaby, but now it was a trouble sound, like Mom's voice when she threatened to whup somebody.

I humped up by the window that looked down the branch and the little road, and often Mom or Dad, or Mallie or one of the boys, would stop walking the floor and stand behind me and watch too. Finally then, Dad and Wilmer went out to get in kindling and coal for the morning, and I sploshed along behind them with the littlest coal bucket. The coal pile was in the back corner of the yard and going there and back I got wet as water with the cold stinging rain soaking right through the old overall jacket Mom put on my head.

Back in the house I could hear Mallie banging around fixing to start supper, rattling the stove lids trying to make out like it wasn't so bad.

'Ah now, they've stopped for the night somewheres. No use'n looking any more for them this day. Go on to milk, Mom. They're setting right now by Uncle Ely's fireplace roasting their shins, better off'n you'll be in that old leaky barn. Hurry back now, supper'll be ready.'

Mom drooped off into the rain toward the barn. Mom is short and round and she always was known to look jolly. But as I watched her then as she moved slowly up the wet gray hill, her form huddled under the old man-coat she wore, the thought came to me that she looked like a big bundle of worry. Or at least how a bundle of worry ought to look if you could see it.

I helped Mallie get supper and we had it on the table when Mom got back from the milking, and we all settled around the long table. Every time anybody spoke it was wondering something about the girls, but it was scattered talk even so.

All of a sudden I jerked my head up and listened. 'I hear singing!' I was off to the window like a shot, pressing my nose flat to the pane, but it was dark out and not a thing to be seen. Mom was behind me, and Dad behind Mom, wiping his mouth and not believing. 'The young un's daft now! Now who'd be singing on a night like this, out in the rain there?' But his voice got mighty lively. Mallie went about the table in a calm way setting down four more plates. The singing became a tune, not one that we knew, then we could make out words.

A branch of May I will bring you, my love,
Here at your door I stand —

Mom got to the door and yanked it open so that it banged against the wall, and I don't know whether the rain blew in and hit her in the face or whether she was crying. There was a great laughing and scrambling and tumbling in at the door. Jewel's arm stuck up through the mess of them, and she was holding up a dripping dogwood branch and hollering, 'Happy May Day!'

Four wetter, sorrier-looking humans you never did see. They just fell down in a heap before the fire and I swear there wasn't a dry thread on them. Their hair and their clothes were plastered right tight to their skin, and what was left of the shoes on their feet made big sloshing noises and left little rivers from the door to the fireplace. They said they had walked the three days solid, stopping to shelter under cliffs now and then when the rain got too hard, and they had taken up for the two nights at houses of people they knew along the way.

I reckon they were just about dead. But our house had come to life in two shakes of a sheep's tail. More supper had to be cooked, bath water carried and set to heat on the stove. Everybody had to hug and kiss the girls for all they were wringing wet, and fuss at them and ask questions. And they had to tell over and over what a terrible time they had getting home. Each one of them had her own way of telling the tale, so you might have thought they had made four separate trips.

They got dry clothes on and we rubbed the most of the water out of their hair, then at last we all got around the table again. The girls were so drowsy they had a hard time staying awake to eat, but were too worked up to go to sleep either. They chattered away like a flock of bluebirds.

'We were just so tired we didn't see how we'd ever in the world come that last mile or two,' said Patty. 'But when we did get in sight of the house, Edna said we mustn't go in acting sick, and worry you all to death and maybe get a whupping for traveling in the rain. So we commenced hollering and laughing to get our spirits up, and then Pauline broke a limb off of a dogwood tree we passed —'

'And Jewel grabbed it out of my hand and waved it around in the air and began leading us out in the May Carol — '

'I didn't think I recognized that tune,' Mom said.

'It's a song we sing at school on May Day morning and it's the prettiest thing!' Edna cried. 'But let's not sing tonight, we're all too tired and hoarse. Tomorrow. And tomorrow I aim to make the best cake — I learnt how at school. It's called Grandmother's Butter Cake — '

'And I'll make a goulash,' Patty offered.

'And we'll *all* plant corn,' Dad sounded stern, then looked sheepish and added, 'if it ain't too wet.' We all laughed at that because we knew it'd take three or four good days for the ground to dry up enough for any corn planting.

I climbed up on the big featherbed in the next room and stuck my head in under the quilts and said my prayers where no one would see me. I wanted to get down on my knees and pray like you're supposed to, but I was afraid someone would come in through the door. I told God thank-you for watching over the girls on their trip. I prayed some other things, and then a special prayer that the night would pass fast so tomorrow would be here, and so on until I let my mind drift onto so many matters that I forgot I was praying, just kept on thinking hopeful thoughts and clear left off saying Amen.

Not too many tomorrows and tomorrows away from now, I'd be going off to school too, and be having great adventures, and be learning new ways. The rain was coming down harder now on the tin roof, but it hadn't ever sung a sweeter song — or maybe I was getting it mixed up with the girls' voices. I guess they couldn't wait for tomorrow after all, to sing thankfulness for home and family. By the time they got to the last lines, 'God bless you all both great and small, and send you a joyful May!' the song and the singing had become a part of my dreams.

> I've been a-wand'ring all the night,
>   And the best part of the day,

And when I come back home again
I will bring you a branch of May.

A branch of May I will bring you, my love,
Here at your door I stand;

I've been a-wan-d'ring all the night, And the best part of the day, And when I come back home a-gain I will bring you a branch of May.

It's nothing but a sprout, but it's well budded out
By the work of the Lord's own hand.

In my pocket I've got a purse
Tied up with a silver string,
All that I do need is a bit of silver
To line it well within!

My song is done and I must be gone,
For I can no longer stay;
God bless you all, both great and small
And send you a joyful May.

Mallie says that the day the railroad train came through the whole family and everybody for miles around gathered up to watch.

'The excitement started a long time before that day, though. Ever since the men building the railroad had come one day and talked to Granddaddy Hall, the talk amongst the folks around was a wonder to hear. Before the men actually came, no one set much store by the scattern tales spread about, that a railroad was coming through Perry County, and not even the young folks believed that it would come right through Viper, right in sight of our house.

'But then the building men came, in their old dirty clothes, came up and asked Grandpa could they make a little settlement there on his land till the road went through. In no time atall there were a whole passel of little slab houses in the bottom across the branch from us, close to where Aunt Maggie lives now. The men lived there and worked the road, folks got to calling their settlement Slabtown, and now some fifty years later, this end of Viper still carries that name.

'They paid people big money for land for the right of way, and you never saw such a hoo-raw in our parts. Old people grumbled and growled and said the road would be the ruination of the country; young folks couldn't wait to see the first train come up the track, and to ride on it, young foolhardy things. But argue and say whatever they would, the railroad men didn't care, they went off out of sight every day down the river around the curve and young uns played amongst their slab houses. Every day we'd listen to hear the blasting and hammering folks said the men had to do to make the railroad. Then one day the loud scary boom-booming sounded far away, and a few days later we could even hear the hammers ring on the steel.

'Mom wouldn't talk about letting us girls go off down the road to watch, though I was pretty near woman grown by then. Used to make me awful mad that she'd let Raymond and Truman go and them younger'n I was. Finally though the work moved around the curve and I could watch them in the distance, could hear the rackety steam drill, go rack-rack-rack all day, could hear them hammering and could see the hammers and the steel rails flash in the sunshine, could hear the men hollering like they's forever cussing one another out, and sometimes they'd sing to their work on the rails. The boys, they'd come home and they'd play like they'd be railroad men. They'd get Pa's old sledge hammer he used around the anvil to make horseshoes and the like with, and they'd come down on the anvil, WHANG! WHANG! TE-WHANG! and try to sing out like the men.

'Lot of the boys around used to hang about the men's shacks of an evening, listen to their talk and their songs. Those men loved to sing, only they didn't seem to know any of the songs that we did. The music they made there at Slabtown was most all of it blustery and loud, songs about railroading, like "Casey Jones" and "John Henry." Wasn't long fore the boys of a Sunday, sitting around with their banjers, were singing "John Henry" as pyert as you please, like they'd been singing it a hundred years.

John Henry was a little baby boy
A-setting on his daddy's knee,
He wropped his fist around a little piece of steel,
Said, steel'll be the death of me, Lordie babe,
Steel'll be the death of me.

John Hen-ry had a pretty little woman, she followed him a-round all the time. She didn't know the win-ter from the sum-mer time, and the green leaves a hangin' on the vine, Lordie babe, green leaves a - hangin' on the vine.

John Henry had a pretty little woman,
She followed him around all the time;
She didn't know the winter from the summertime
And the green leaves a-hangin on the vine, Lordie babe,
Green leaves a-hangin on the vine.

They took John Henry to the mountain top
He looked to the Lord above,
Said, take this hammer and wrap it up in gold
And give it to the woman I love, Lordie babe,
Give it to the woman I love.

They took his hammer and wropped it up in gold,
And give it to Polly Ann,
And the very last words she heard him say
Was, Polly, do the best that you can, Lordie babe,
Polly, do the best that you can.

'At last the day came and word went round that they were going to bring the steam locomotive around the curve and up past our house to try out the new track. That morning we all ate breakfast fast and Mom wrapped up the baby and we all went down to the new track. Everybody in the country was there with all of their young uns. Storekeepers and school-teachers too. Wouldn't of done any good to try to keep school anyway, that day.

'Mom wouldn't let us near get as close as we wanted to. Every woman had some child or other trying to hold it back from the dangerous track. Then here came some of the men and they put up ropes and said not a soul was to get beyond them, and the men strung out down the track and they com-menced hollering something, all the way down the line around the curve, to the next man and him to the next, out of sight, and then we heard it holler. Gee-oh! Went like a wild panther screaming in the woods someplace. The little babies started to cry, some of them, but that was nothing like the way they took on when that big thing came in sight and commenced rolling down that track right at us. Children and some of the plum grown people went scattern back through the crowd, getting as far away as they could, and still see. Some of the women had to take their babies away off out of sight, they got so scared.

'Gee-oh! That was the biggest, ugliest, awfullest-looking thing! The noise she made was enough to take the wits out of you, let alone the terrible looks of her. Put me in a mind of something alive, something big and black and — HANTY! Fire just a-working out of the insides of her, smoke just a-billern out of that big black funnel on her top. Her chuffing and screaming like something had give her a mortal wound. Bells a-clanging, men a-hollern, women and children a-screaming, young boys a-laughing. It was all I could do to keep still and not run. Lordy mercy, what a time!

'Well, it was the coal you know, that the trains come in after. These hills right sticking full of coal, or else the L. & N. would never have come in away here. Wouldn't a day pass after that but what five or six big long trainloads of coal would rumble by. Then no time passed before they went to hauling out lumber and livestock and such on the freight trains. Then they sent the short dog on the tracks, too, for people to travel on. Daytime and nighttime, every day, and they didn't stop for Sunday, those big lumbering trains kept the rails hot.

'It sure was an awful exciting noise, whenever a train went by. We could see it right plain from our house, through several gaps in the trees down along the river there. You could hear them coming a long ways down the line, and that's when we all of us young uns would break for the front porch, least ones'd have to be h'isted up by us bigger ones and we'd all wave and holler at the trainmen in the engine. Not that they could hear us, but sometimes they'd see us, and wave back.

'They brought a sight of work in here too, the railroads. Raymond he got a big job, railroad operator in the station, Truman went to work in the big company commissary in

Kenmont Holler when the mine opened up there, and all the men that wanted to could get a job down in the mines. Gee-oh! How fast things around here did change. Money circulating free and easy, everybody traveling to far-off places on the excursion trains. Great big fellers, never been off their place before, go on that excursion to Natural Bridge, Kentucky, come back thinking they'd been to the end of the world. Come back talking proper and sassing their grannies like John down the river there did. But I reckon though that the railroad was a good thing.'

I can't remember as far back as Mallie can. The fact is, when I was born, the trains had been rolling by so long that everybody had got used to them, thought nothing extra of them. But one thing made a big mark on my mind, and that was Truman's job in the commissary. For he would bring home the oddest things. One night he came in grinning and set down his poke, told us to look in it and see if we knew what that was. Mom took out a little tin can with a picture of a cow on it, said 'Evaporated Milk.' She opened it up and we got a spoon each and passed it around, and that was the funniest-tasting stuff. Some of them couldn't stand it, but I loved it. It was smooth and thick and sort of sweeter than Old Bill's cream tasted. I stole the can out of the cupboard after supper and went into one of the dark rooms and drank about half of what was left, it was so good, and I got so I would do that every time Truman'd bring a can of store cream.

Mom would fuss whenever he'd spend money on stuff to eat like that. 'Now Lord Truman, what'd you go and bring me beans in a tin can for? We got the same thing in the cellar, canned two hundred quarts of beans this fall and he brings home beans! And fruit cake! Ain't my fruit cake good enough for you? You'd better save your money, stead of spending it on tids and tads, sir.'

He must have saved up his money some way because one day he drove up home in a new car. To me it looked as big as a train, and it was sky blue. I thought it was the most beautiful and the finest thing I ever saw, and I was proud of our family for having a car. Truman spent the rest of the day taking carloads of us riding in the car, down the rocky branch and in under the railroad trestle and down the county road toward Jeff. That road was dusty and narrow and sometimes it curved sharp around on high banks, and he brought me back covered with dust and scared to death, but I don't know when I have ever felt so grand since. Then Dad got in and said he aimed to drive it. Truman showed him how to start and sat beside him, and Dad said looked like there wasn't a thing to it. The words weren't out of his mouth before that machine gave a lunge and Dad went tearing off. But not in the road; he plum missed that and headed the car right over into the branch. He went splitting the waters through the shallow parts and landed ka-whooshle with the front end nosed down into the Big Hole, Dad hollering 'Stop her! Stop her!' every breath. He threw the door open and waded the water up to his knees to get away. Said he'd be blast if he'd ever monkey with driving a fool thing like that again, and to my knowledge he never did.

Granny was scandalized when she heard about the car, and it was for a long time that she wouldn't ride in it. I have heard her say to Mom, 'Lordy mercy, Abbie, why the way them contraptions fly 'long they'll kill a body. Why they must go fifteen or twenty mile an hour! Not me, no sir, you just give me a good gentle nag and I'll get there not fur behind you, and I'll not have the life scared out of my body, to boot.'

Well, that was in 1929, the year of the Big Flood. Truman kept the car out beside our cow house, in a little dry holler that runs out of the hillside there. That night when it began to rain Mom tried to wake him up to go move the car, because she had known that holler to wash a lot of trash down, and it might dirty up the car, and besides if it kept on raining like it was there might even be some danger of the car's washing clear away. But Truman was fast asleep; it was always hard to rouse him, and so he just wouldn't get up. Then there was something we found out later was a cloudburst. Thunder ripped open the yellow heavens and the mighty waters fell on us not in drops, not in sheets, but all at once. I always had liked to think that when God wanted us to have rain, He'd take a water bucket and sprinkle the earth with His hand. I remember thinking that night that somebody in our neighborhood must've made God mighty mad, for I could see Him snatching up the biggest bucket He had, a mile wide and ten miles deep, and just turning it upside down on our little holler, Him roaring and bellering away all the time. It was awesome.

Of course, the car was the first thing to go. Truman and Raymond, they shot out of bed as soon as they heard that hard rain hit the roof, and they beat their way out to the car and tried to save her but they heard a racket, looked up the mountain side, and there was a great wall of water and rocks and trees just boiling and tumbling down that dry holler straight for them. They barely got out of the way of it, and as it was they were half drowned when they did get in on the porch. The whole family stood with them there in our night clothes and watched the beautiful car make its last ride. The lightning made a steady bright light for us to see by. She bucked the waters like something alive, whirled about, stood on her nose, scraped along on her side, rolled along upright and easy a minute; then she struck the rock in the Big Hole and we could hear the scrunching of her sides giving in; finally, she sank from sight.

Just then the main branch sent down a wall of water and in it was all kinds of things like trees and chicken houses with scared squawking hens on top, and great logs someone had sawed to build a house. Dad and Wilmer just did get the cows out of the cow house and then the huge old square-log building went breaking itself to pieces down the branch, many of the logs just missing the porch where we stood. In the middle of everything Mom hollered out in a dying voice, 'There goes my bread tray! My good long bread tray!' and everybody laughed. We decided to leave the house and go out around the hill to Ollie's. Her house was on high ground and nothing would hurt it. They bundled me up and Edna and Truman took turns carrying me, and we strung out in a long line with the lightning and one coal-oil lantern to show the way around the slipping, giving hill above our house. Mallie noticed Pauline carrying a little bit of a bundle, some things knotted up into one of Dad's red handkerchiefs. Mallie asked her what on earth she had got there. Pauline was crying. 'It's my clothes,' she said.

Our house didn't wash away, but it came in a hair of it. What Granny Katty said about the flood made me wonder if she had the same thought I did about God and the water buckets. She said to Truman that the flood was a judgment sent on him on account of his pride in driving about in that sinful contraption.

We heard about the radio for a long time before we ever saw one, but the day that my brother Raymond brought one in home, that was a day we all remember. That was one day I was mad because we had such a big family. I *never* got to have the earphones. I was the least one and so naturally I had to be last in everything, but this was even worse, because we tuned in on 'Amos 'n Andy,' and the ones that had the earphones first would want to know what was happening since they listened and they'd snatch them back again. Everybody was laughing and slapping their knees and telling what the radio was saying, and I couldn't understand a word of it because every time I'd reach for the gear someone else would snatch it away and clap it on his own head. Finally I commenced to holler and Mom took the things off of Raymond's head and fitted them down over my ears.

'What you hear, now? Tell us quick, what they saying?'

'Well . . . well . . . it's somebody singing, like, "Is I blue! Is I blue!" '

'Let me hear, let me hear it now!' Dad grabbed the earphones.

After a while we made up some rules about the earphones. Dad would listen to the news and tell us all. We took time about listening to the stories, and whoever listened had to tell anyone else who wanted to know, what was going on. Dad or the boys could listen to ball games all they liked, nobody among the womenfolks was interested. Pauline and Jewel were crazy about the songs they heard through the earphones, and they had to listen and learn them and sing them so we could tell whether we liked them or not.

They were getting to be all the fashion, those radio songs. The young folks went around singing 'Pale Wildwood Flower' and 'Zeb Turney's Girl' and 'Sweet Fern.' Hillbilly songs, the radio called this music, and it claimed that these songs were sung all through the mountains, but we never had heard anything just like them before. I guess if it hadn't been for the radio it's no telling how long it would have taken us to find out that we were hillbillies, or what kind of songs we were supposed to sing. But the radio soon fixed all that. It got to be that if you asked any young person to sing 'Barbry Ellen,' whoever it was would look at you and laugh and look ashamed of you. 'That old-fashioned thing? Why I don't even remember how that goes, it's been so long.' And he'd begin to twang away on a steel guitar and start out on one of the radio songs, singing 'through his nose' like the hillbillies on the programs did. Or, if it was someone that got mad at being called a hillbilly, who took all this talk about hillbillies as a personal insult, he'd be likely to say, ' "Barbry Ellen"? Why folks laugh at you if you sing that old thing. Call you a hillbilly.' And then he'd sing 'After the Ball Is Over,' a high-class song, a city song. Then, I remember the girls around just older than me, who thought they were old enough to be sparking the boys, they'd shut their eyes and frown up their faces to look sad, and they'd sing that song 'Pale Wildwood Flower,' which was such a popular love song on the radio then.

O I'll twine and I'll mingle my waving black hair
With the roses so red and the lilies so fair,
And the pinks and the daisies that grow in the dell
It's all for my true love, he loves me so well.

– 248 –

O, I'll twine and I'll mingle my waving black hair with the
ros - es so red and the li - lies so fair, And the
pinks and the dai - sies that grow in the dell, It's
all for my true love, he loves me so well.

O you taught me to love you and promised to love
And to think of me always all others above;
But you've loved and you've left me in one fleeting hour,
Gone and forgotten your pale wildwood flower.

And so in my mind the songs all got mixed and tangled until
I came to think on the hillbilly songs and the old songs as the
same kind of thing, got ashamed to be caught singing either
kind, got to liking the slick city music on the radio the best,
and I guess most everybody else did likewise. Anyway, I
remember a time, some few years there, when we in our family
didn't near sing our own songs like we used to.

We didn't sing much of anything, though, come to think
of it, old songs or new. There got to be so many different things
to do and so many places to go, and the radio programs to
listen to, and the talking machine, and so on, that we just about
quit gathering to talk and sing. Truman twanged around on a
steel guitar for a while, and I remember his favorite song was
'Daisies Won't Tell' — he was courting to marry round about
that time. Wilmer learned to fiddle a little, from Dad. It hurts
my ears yet to think of his bow screaking out 'Zeb Turney's
Girl.'

Then the missionaries came, in cars and on the trains and in buses. They came mostly from out around Illinois and they started preaching what the Old Regulars called newfangled religion. 'I never saw the beat of how they carry on,' I heard one of the Old Regular preachers say to Dad after meeting one Sunday. The missionaries had just made a start then and some of the old folks thought they were butting in where they had no business; and of course the old mountain church felt challenged in its ability to meet the people's needs, and in its very doctrine. A lot of the old heads got mad and talked among themselves, like this preacher I started to tell about. He said to Dad:

'Why you know, Balis, it's crazy what they a-doing. A-saving little tiny young uns don't know their own mind. Thertning and begging them. Plum agin the Bible that is, Bible says you have to reach the age of accountability before you can make the choice. Church can't take in babies! And Sunday schools! Where in the Bible can you find where it exhorts you to send your young uns to Sunday school? Them young preachers better grow up a little and study God's Book and kind of meller down in His Will, that's what it takes to preach.

'And do you know what they do? Ben's wife Sallie said she come around a curve on two of them young women the other day and they had cameras and they'uz down taking a picture of a mud hole! Wasn't a living soul having his picture took, just a mud hole. She said she laughed and asked them what in tarnation they'uz taking a picture of a mud hole for, and they said they'uz making some photographs so they could show the people back out in Illinois what the countryside here was like. Why don't you know they're just down in here to make fun of us?'

But the missionaries stayed, and by and by the two churches settled their differences and got along pretty well with each other. We young folks liked to go to the Sunday schools and the missionary services. The teachers were young, happy looking people, and their church was a lot livelier than Mom's church. Their songs were snappy and easy to sing, some you could almost have danced to if they hadn't been religious. The missionaries built houses all up and down the hollers, and then churches too. In Viper during one summer nearly all the young folks around came forward and shook the preacher's hand and said they wanted to be saved, while everybody sang, 'Just As I Am, Without One Plea.' It was a big revival. I was among the first to go up. I was sixteen years old.

Otherwise, that was a kind of a low time, the year I was sixteen. Especially at home it was sad. It wasn't anything you could name, just that all of a sudden everything familiar about living was gone. Folks around all seemed restless — they just couldn't be satisfied. I would catch myself getting that feeling too, many a time, and I'd puzzle about why it should be. Maybe because the house was so empty, just me and Mom and Dad there.

Most of the others were married and living off to themselves now. Unie and May had married men who took them away off, Unie to Boston, Massachusetts, and May to North Carolina, so that we hardly ever saw them anymore. Those who weren't married were off in college or teaching school and boarding away from home. Mom worried about them all scattered about that way, and she spent the night hours writing letters at the kitchen table. For the first time I began to notice that she was getting old, and Dad too, both white headed and stoop shouldered.

Dad couldn't make the crop any more, for he wasn't able with no one to help him. I hated hoeing corn but now sometimes I actually longed for the cornfield with the whole crowd of us working there together. I longed for the house to be chug full and running over with people and racket and laughing and singing. How bad it was to be the baby of the family and see them all go off and leave you just as you get big enough to take your own part and talk among them like a grown person! Seemed like nowadays, as soon as a boy or girl got half grown he went off somewheres and got a job or married.

No one stayed and settled down in Perry County anymore, in spite of the railroad and the mines.

I was mighty busy that year; we had a big new high school in Viper and I was finishing up my schooling there, and our church was growing and having all kinds of meetings and picnics and things, and I was walking some with the boys now, though I was still about the most bashful thing that ever lived. There was something to do every minute but yet there was a lonesomeness that hung over the hills and made my heart ache.

And there was still another trouble, and this one I could name. All my life up to now, I had dreamed and longed and schemed to leave home, to go places like the others, but now that the time was coming near, I hated the thoughts of getting through high school, was scared to death of the time when I too would have to go away. It was like a big Something was pushing me out of the house, down the branch, and off onto the railroad trains when I didn't want to go. I wished I could start getting younger instead of older; I wished I could do something about the calendar so that December wouldn't come and bring my birthday, so that I could always and forever be sixteen.

The long warm evenings were somehow the saddest of all. We'd get our bit of supper over and the work done up, the cow milked and the horse and pigs and chickens fed, the coal and kindling in. Then we'd sit around in the front room, I'd get my lessons and Mom would piece quilts or mend, Dad would maybe take down the dulcimer off the wall and make the old tunes ring proud in the still, forsaken night. Have you ever heard a dulcimer played on a still soft night by a lonesome person?

One such night, late in the month of May, we were sitting like this. The dulcimer was crying and the moon was rising in a spring mist, and the lonesomeness moved down from the hills and sat with us. The seven-fifteen short dog moaned by, blowing for the crossing. It was a night like a hundred other nights, with us sitting there, working and talking a little, humming and thinking to ourselves.

About fifteen minutes after the train passed, car lights turned up the branch. Mom said as it was her habit, 'Now, wonder who that could be yonder.' Dad went out on the porch to watch the lights come near, to try to see who might be passing by. The lights went out, the motor turned off, white and dark shapes got out at all the doors, talking, laughing, whispering, moving up to our house and up the steps. Dad said, 'Come right in. Who is it now? Well-l-l, for the good Lord — where, when — how did *you* get here!'

May's voice whooped out between all the hugging and kissing. 'We aimed to surprise you! Drove all the way today. Reckon you can put us all up at one time?' May and Leon and the three children and Mallie, who was staying with May then. What a time! We all flew round, building up a fire in the kitchen stove and putting supper on. May looked around her. 'Am I the first one home?' she asked, and then just grinned when we asked what she meant.

Well, at that, Leon pulled out and went up to the train station, just to see who he could see, he said, and he came back in five minutes, and said, 'I picked up two tramps on the road and they want a place to stay all night!' Out of the car rolled Kitty and Edna, come home unexpectedly from their schools. They had come in on the train and had started walking down from the station. People just kept coming then, Jewel from Berea College and Pauline from Science Hill School and Wilmer from Lee's College down the line in Jackson. And about midnight Unie landed in, all the way from Massachusetts.

Next morning the ones who lived in around close, Raymond and Truman and their families, from Kenmont Holler, and Ollie and Roy and their seven, from around the hill, all gathered in, and the family was complete.

The children told us how it came about. They got to writing around among themselves, how much they'd like to make a trip home, how low Mom's letters sounded, how Dad had cut his hand bad again with the ax, how the little ones all wanted to see their Grandma and Grandpa and meet up with each other, how the mountains were so pretty in the springtime . . . So they all made it up to come in home on the same day, let it be a surprise to us at home, have a reunion.

Some came to stay a month, some to stay a week, and the college students just for the week end. But it began with the first night we were all together again, the *right* feeling. I felt it first after supper was by, along toward the edge of dark, when we drifted by ones and by twos out onto the front porch.

The memory of that evening always makes me feel happy and warm. All of us there, full of love for each other, the brave little moon breaking at last through the mist, helped by thousands of lightning bugs, the clear twinkly laughing of the branch, and the way our voices sounded as we talked quietly the ways of our lives. The sudden sharp slamming of the screen door across the branch at Aunt Maggie's and the far-off wail of the train whistle that set the dogs to barking and howling for miles around. Little fights over who was going to sit in the swing, or beside of Grandma.

Best of all the singing. When we all got started on 'The Cuckoo She's a Pretty Bird,' we sang back all the happy days and ways of our growing up. Remembrances by the score swept over my mind. Funny happenings, happy days and sad days, and I could tell by the sound of the other voices that they were remembering too. The lovely past was not gone, it had just been shut up inside of a song!

Inside of a hundred songs, I should say. We sang on and on, till the moon was middleways the sky, and still we had not sung them all. I was sitting in my old place wedged in between Mom and Edna in the swing, and I had a strange nice feeling of being a baby again with them all around to fuss at me and boss and love me, but at the same time I felt grown-up and wise. I knew a thing now that I wondered if the others had ever thought of. I knew that no matter how far apart we might scatter the world over, that we'd still be the Ritchie Family as long as we lived and sang the same old songs, and that the songs would live as long as there was a family.

The cuc-koo she's a pretty bird, she sings as she flies, She
brings us glad tid - ings, and she tells us no lies.

The cuckoo she's a pretty bird,
She sings as she flies;
She brings us glad tidings,
And she tells us no lies.
　　She sucks all pretty flowers
　　To make her voice clear,
　　And she never sings Cuckoo
　　Till the spring of the year.

Come all you young women,
Take warning by me:
Never place your affections
On the love of a man;
　　For the roots they will wither,
　　The branches decay;
　　He'll turn his back on you
　　And he'll walk square away.

If you do forsake me
I'll not be foresworn,
And they'll all be mistaken
If they think that I'll mourn;
　　For I'll get myself up in
　　Some right high degree,
　　And I'll walk as light by him
　　As he does by me.

O the cuckoo she's a pretty bird,
She sings as she flies;
She brings us glad tidings,
She tells us no lies.
　　She sucks all pretty flowers
　　To make her voice clear,
　　And she never says Cuckoo
　　Till the spring of the year.

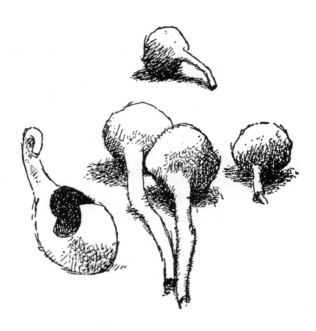

Index of Songs